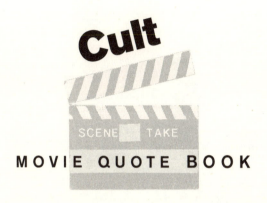

# Cult

## SCENE TAKE

## MOVIE QUOTE BOOK

**MJF BOOKS**
New York

Published by MJF Books
Fine Communications
322 Eighth Avenue
New York, NY 10001

*Cult Movie Quote Book*
LC Control Number 2007941359
ISBN-13: 978-1-56731-909-5
ISBN-10: 1-56731-909-2

Copyright © 2005 NICOTEXT

This edition is published by MJF Books in arrangement with the
Lennart Sane Agency AB, Sweden.

Printed in the United States of America.

Designed by Lisa Chovnick

MJF Books and the MJF colophon are trademarks of Fine Creative Media, Inc.

QM   10   9   8   7   6   5   4   3   2   1

"I must be crazy to be in a loony bin like this."

— ONE FLEW OVER THE CUCKOO'S NEST

– I haven't got a brain . . . only straw.
– How can you talk if you haven't got a brain?
– I don't know. But some people without brains
do an awful lot of talking, don't they?
– Yes, I guess you're right.

It had been a wonderful evening and what I needed now, to give it
the perfect ending, was a little of the Ludwig Van.

You're gonna need a bigger boat.

– It's got a cop motor, a 440 cubic inch plant, it's got cop tires,
cop suspensions, cop shocks. It's a model made before catalytic converters
so it'll run good on regular gas. What do you say,
is it the new Bluesmobile or what?
– Fix the cigarette lighter.

When a naked man is chasing a woman through an
alley with a butcher's knife and a hard-on, I figure
he isn't out collecting for the Red Cross!

I don't give a good fuck what you know or don't know.
I'm going to torture you anyway, regardless.

## THE WIZARD OF OZ 1939, USA
**Director:** Victor Fleming
**Cast:** Judy Garland, Ray Bolger, Bert Lahr
**Screenplay:** Noel Langley, Florence Ryerson and Edgar Allan Woolf
*Based on the book by L. Frank Baum*

## A CLOCKWORK ORANGE 1971, USA
**Director:** Stanley Kubrick
**Cast:** Malcolm McDowell, Patrick Magee, Adrienne Corri
**Screenplay:** Stanley Kubrick *Based on the book by Anthony Burgess*

## JAWS 1975, USA
**Director:** Steven Spielberg
**Cast:** Roy Scheider, Robert Shaw, Richard Dreyfuss
**Screenplay:** Peter Benchley, Carl Gottlieb, John Milius, Howard Sackler
and Robert Shaw *Based on the book by Peter Benchley*

## THE BLUES BROTHERS 1980, USA
**Director:** John Landis
**Cast:** John Belushi, Dan Aykroyd, Cab Calloway
**Screenplay:** Dan Aykroyd and John Landis

## DIRTY HARRY 1971, USA
**Director:** Don Siegal
**Cast:** Clint Eastwood, Harry Guardino, Reni Santoni
**Screenplay:** Harry Julian Fink, Rita M. Fink, Dean Riesner and John Milius

## RESERVOIR DOGS 1992, USA
**Director:** Quentin Tarantino
**Cast:** Harvey Keitel, Tim Roth, Michael Madsen
**Screenplay:** Roger Avary and Quentin Tarantino

You call yourself a free spirit, a wild thing, and you're terrified somebody's gonna stick you in a cage. Well, baby, you're already in that
cage. You built it yourself. And it's not bounded in the west by Tulip,
Texas, or in the east by Somali-land. It's wherever you go. Because no
matter where you run, you just end up running into yourself.


– When people think you're dying, they really, really listen to you,
instead of just . . .
– instead of just waiting for their turn to speak?


They'll talk to ya and talk to ya and talk to ya about individual
freedom. But they see a free individual, it's gonna scare 'em.


I can remember when I was a little boy. My grandmother and I could
hold conversations entirely without ever opening our mouths.


If I have any more fun today I don't think I can take it!


– We got a secret weapon. God is our co-pilot!
–You'll need him!
– God is our co-pilot?
– Uh huh . . .
– Remember our car?
– Uh huh . . .
– Two seats?
– Two seats . . .
– Where's he gonna sit?

## BREAKFAST AT TIFFANY'S 1961, USA
**Director:** Blake Edwards
**Cast:** Audrey Hepburn, George Peppard
**Screenplay:** Truman Capote, George Axelrod

## FIGHT CLUB 1999, USA
**Director:** David Fincher  **Cast:** Brad Pitt, Edward Norton, Helena Bonham Carter
**Screenplay:** Jim Uhls  *Based on the book by Chuck Palahniuk*

## EASY RIDER 1969, USA
**Director:** Dennis Hopper  **Cast:** Peter Fonda, Dennis Hopper, Jack Nicholson.
**Screenplay:** Peter Fonda, Dennis Hopper and Terry Southern

## THE SHINING 1980, USA
**Director:** Stanley Kubrick  **Cast:** Jack Nicholson, Shelley Duvall, Danny Lloyd
**Screenplay:** Stanley Kubrick and Diane Johnson  *Based on the book by Stephen King*

## THE TEXAS CHAINSAW MASSACRE 1974, USA
**Director:** Tobe Hopper  **Cast:** Marilyn Burns, Gunnar Hansen, Ed Neal
**Screenplay:** Kim Henkel and Tobe Hooper

## THE CANNONBALL RUN 1981, USA
**Director:** Hal Needham
**Cast:** Burt Reynolds, Roger Moore, Farrah Fawcett
**Screenplay:** Brock Yates

– I can't make out whether you're a
bloody madman or just half-witted.
– I have the same problem, sir.

– Is there someone inside you?
– Sometimes.
– Who is it?
– I don't know.
– Is it Captain Howdy?
– I don't know.
– If I ask him to tell me, will you let him answer?
– No!
– Why not?
– I'm afraid.

How do you explain school to a higher intelligence?

This is a snakeskin jacket! And for me it's a symbol of my
individuality, and my belief . . . in personal freedom.

– Look at your algebra book. It looks like it's never even been opened!
– I only use it on special equations.

"More human than human" is our motto.

## LAWRENCE OF ARABIA 1962, United Kingdom
**Director:** David Lean  **Cast:** Peter O'Toole, Alec Guinness, Anthony Quinn
**Screenplay:** T.E. Lawrence, Robert Bolt and Michael Wilson

## EXORCIST, THE  1973, USA
**Director:** William Friedkin
**Cast:** Ellen Burstyn, Max von Sydow, Linda Blair
**Screenplay:** William Peter Blatty

## E.T. THE EXTRA-TERRESTRIAL 1982, USA
**Director:** Steven Spielberg  **Cast:** Dee Wallace, Henry Thomas, Peter Coyote
**Screenplay:** Melissa Mathison

## WILD AT HEART 1990, USA
**Director:** David Lynch  **Cast:** Nicolas Cage, Laura Dern, Diane Ladd
**Screenplay:** David Lynch  *Based on the book by Barry Gifford*

## ROCK 'N' ROLL HIGH SCHOOL 1979, USA
**Director:** Allan Arkush, Joe Dante  **Cast:** P.J. Soles, Vincent Van Patten, Clint Howard
**Screenplay:** Richard Whitley, Russ Dvonch

## BLADE RUNNER 1982, USA
**Director:** Ridley Scott  **Cast:** Harrison Ford, Rutger Hauer, Sean Young
**Screenplay:** Hampton Fancher, David Webb Peoples, Roland Kibbee
*Based on the book by Philip K. Dick*

John Connor gave me a picture of you once. I didn't know why at the time. It was very old, torn-faded. You were young like you are now. You seemed just a little sad. I used to always wonder what you were thinking at that moment. I memorized every line, every curve. I came across time for you, Sarah, I love you, I always have.

I think someone should just take this city and just . . . just flush it down the fuckin' toilet.

– I don't think about that much with one shot anymore, Mike.
– You have to think about one shot. One shot is what it's all about. A deer's gotta be taken with one shot.

1,000 British soldiers have been massacred. While I stood here talking peace, a war has started.

I am not an elephant! I am not an animal! I am a human being! I am a man!

Cherry was right. You're soft, you should have let 'em kill me, 'cause I'm gonna kill you. I'll catch up with ya. I don't know when, but I'll catch up. Every time you turn around, expect to see me, 'cause one time you'll turn around and I'll be there. I'm gonna kill ya, Matt.

## THE TERMINATOR 1984, USA
**Director:** James Cameron
**Cast:** Arnold Schwartzenegger, Michael Biehn, Linda Hamilton
**Screenplay:** James Cameron, Gale Anne Hurd, William Wisher Jr.
    and Harlan Ellison

## TAXI DRIVER 1976, USA
**Director:** Martin Scorsese
**Cast:** Robert De Niro, Cybill Shepherd, Harvey Keitel
**Screenplay:** Paul Schrader

## THE DEER HUNTER 1978, USA
**Director:** Michael Cimino
**Cast:** Robert De Niro, Christopher Walken, Meryl Streep
**Screenplay:** Michael Cimino, Louis Garfinkle, Quinn K. Redeker
    and Deric Washburn

## ZULU 1964, United Kingdom
**Director:** Cy Endfield
**Cast:** Stanley Baker, Jack Hawkins, Ulla Jacobsson
**Screenplay:** John Prebble and Cy Endfield

## THE ELEPHANT MAN 1980, USA
**Director:** David Lynch
**Cast:** Anthony Hopkins, John Hurt, Anne Bancroft
**Screenplay:** Christopher De Vore, Eric Bergren and David Lynch
*Based on the book by Sir Frederick Treves and Ashley Montagu*

## RED RIVER 1948, USA
**Director:** Howard Hawks
**Cast:** John Wayne, Montgomery Clift, Walter Brennan
**Screenplay:** Borden Chase and Charles Schnee

You're not the boss of me, Jack! You're not the king of Dirk!
I'm the boss of me! I'm the king of me. I'm Dirk Diggler!
I'm the star! It's my big dick and I say when we roll!


– How do you feel?
– Fast and loose, man.
– In the gut, I mean.
– I feel tight, but good.


Faster than a speeding bullet! More powerful than a locomotive!
Able to leap tall buildings with a single bound, the infant of Krypton
is now the Man of Steel.


I just wanna know how one becomes a janitor because Andrew
here is very interested in pursuing a career in the custodial arts.


– I can't figure out if you're a detective or a pervert.
– Well, that's for me to know and you to find out.


I don't think it's nice, you laughin'. You see, my mule don't like people
laughing. He gets the crazy idea you're laughin' at him. Now if you
apologize, like I know you're going to, I might convince him that you
really didn't mean it.

## BOOGIE NIGHTS  1997, USA
**Director:** Paul Thomas Anderson
**Cast:** Mark Wahlberg, Burt Reynolds, Julianne Moore
**Screenplay:** Paul Thomas Anderson

## THE HUSTLER  1961, USA
**Director:** Robert Rossen
**Cast:** Paul Newman, Jackie Gleason, Piper Laurie
**Screenplay:** Sidney Carroll and Robert Rossen
*Based on the book by Walter Tevis*

## SUPERMAN  1941, USA
**Director:** Dave Fleischer
**Cast:** Bud Collyer (voice), Joan Alexander (voice)
**Screenplay:** Seymour Kneitel, Joe Shuster

## THE BREAKFAST CLUB  1985, USA
**Director:** John Hughes
**Cast:** Emilio Estevez, Judd Nelson, Molly Ringwald
**Screenplay:** John Hughes

## BLUE VELVET  1986, USA
**Director:** David Lynch
**Cast:** Kyle MacLachlan, Isabella Rossellini, Dennis Hopper
**Screenplay:** David Lynch

## A FISTFUL OF DOLLARS  1964, Italy
**Director:** Sergio Leone
**Cast:** Clint Eastwood, Marianne Koch, Gian Maria Volontè
**Screenplay:** A. Bonzzoni, Victor Andrés Catena

– The 1961 Ferrari 250GT California.
Less than a hundred were made.
My father spent three years restoring this car.
It is his love, it is his passion.
– It is his fault he didn't lock the garage.


A man can convince anyone he's somebody else, but never himself.



Good morning! And in case I don't see ya, good afternoon,
good evening, and good night!



Now, I don't have to tell you good folks what's been happening
in our beloved little town. Sheriff murdered, crops burned, stores
looted, people stampeded, and cattle raped. The time has come
to act, and act fast. I'm leaving.



. . . If I was an imitation, a perfect imitation,
how would you know it was me?



I went to the woods because I wanted to live deliberately.
I wanted to live deep and suck out all the marrow of life . . . to put
to rout all that was not life; and not, when I
came to die, discover that I had not lived.

## FERRIS BUELLER'S DAY OFF 1986, USA
**Director:** John Hughes
**Cast:** Matthew Broderick, Alan Ruck, Mia Sara
**Screenplay:** John Hughes


## THE USUAL SUSPECTS 1995, USA
**Director:** Bryan Singer
**Cast:** Stephen Baldwin, Gabriel Byrne, Chazz Palminteri
**Screenplay:** Christopher McQuarrie

## THE TRUMAN SHOW 1998, USA
**Director:** Peter Weir
**Cast:** Jim Carrey, Laura Linney, Ed Harris
**Screenplay:** Andrew Niccol

## BLAZING SADDLES 1974, USA
**Director:** Mel Brooks
**Cast:** Cleavon Little, Gene Wilder, Harvey Korman
**Screenplay:** Andrew Bergman, Mel Brooks, Richard Pryor, Norman Steinberg
and Alan Uger

## THE THING 1982, USA
**Director:** John Carpenter
**Cast:** Kurt Russell, Richard Dysart, A. Wilford Brimley
**Screenplay:** John W. Campbell Jr. and Bill Lancaster

## DEAD POETS SOCIETY 1989, USA
**Director:** Peter Weir
**Cast:** Robin Williams, Robert Sean Leonard, Ethan Hawke
**Screenplay:** Tom Schulman

Housework is like bad sex. Every time I do it I swear I will never do it again. Until the next time company comes.

– How did you find America?
– Turned left at Greenland.

– Don't you think it would be better if you referred to it as him?
– If you say so.
– Your compassion's overwhelming, doctor.

And now, ladies and gentlemen, before I tell you any more, I'm going to show you the greatest thing your eyes have ever beheld. He was a king and a god in the world he knew, but now he comes to civilization merely a captive—a show to gratify your curiosity . . .

This is paradise, I'm tellin' ya. This town is like a great big pussy jus' waitin' to get fucked.

– I get it. No questions.
– No questions, no lies.
– No questions, no truth, either.

## CAN'T STOP THE MUSIC 1980, USA
**Director:** Nancy Walker
**Cast:** Alex Briley, David Hodo, Glenn Hughes
**Screenplay:** Alan Carr, Bronte Woodard

## A HARD DAY'S NIGHT 1964, United Kingdom
**Director:** Richard Lester
**Cast:** John Lennon, Paul McCartney, Ringo Starr
**Screenplay:** Alun Owen

## HALLOWEEN 1978, USA
**Director:** John Carpenter
**Cast:** Donald Pleasence, Jamie Lee Curtis
**Screenplay:** John Carpenter and Debra Hill

## KING KONG 1933, USA
**Directors:** Merian C. Cooper, Ernest B. Schoedsack
**Cast:** Fay Wray, Robert Armstrong and Bruce Cabot
**Screenplay:** James Ashmore Creelman and Ruth Rose

## SCARFACE 1983, USA
**Director:** Brian De Palma
**Cast:** Al Pacino, Steven Bauer, Michelle Pfeiffer
**Screenplay:** Oliver Stone and Howard Hawks
*Based on the book by Armitage Trail*

## XANADU 1980, USA
**Director:** Robert Greenwald
**Cast:** Olivia Newton-John, Gene Kelly, Michael Beck
**Screenplay:** Richard Christian Danus and Marc Reid Rubel

I see men—sixty, seventy years old breaking their balls to stay fit!
What for? When I die, I want to be sick, not healthy.


Looking at the cake is like looking at the future: until you've tasted it
what do you really know? And then, of course, it's too late.


– So, how long you've been in Mexico?
– A week. I mean a day.
– Well, which is it? A week or a day?
– A weekday.

. . . Choose a future. Choose life . . . But why would I want to do a
thing like that? I chose not to choose life, I choose something
else. And the reasons? There are no reasons. Who needs
reasons when you've got heroin?

You see, in this world there's two kinds of people, my friend: those
with loaded guns and those who dig. You dig.


Remember those posters that said, "Today is the first day of the rest
of your life"? Well, that's true of every day but one—the day you die.

## THE WITCHES OF EASTWICK 1987, USA
**Director:** George Miller
**Cast:** Jack Nicholson, Cher, Susan Sarandon
**Screenplay:** Michael Cristofer
*Based on the book by John Updike*

## EXCALIBUR 1991, USA
**Director:** John Boorman **Cast:** Nicol Williamson, Nigel Terry, Helen Mirren
**Screenplay:** Rospo Pallenberg and John Boorman
*Based on the book by Sir Thomas Malory*

## UP IN SMOKE 1978, USA
**Director:** Lou Adler
**Cast:** Cheech Marin, Tommy Chong, Stacy Keach
**Screenplay:** Tommy Chong and Cheech Marin

## TRAINSPOTTING 1996, United Kingdom
**Director:** Danny Boyle
**Cast:** Ewan McGregor, Ewan Bremmer, Jonny Lee Miller
**Screenplay:** John Hodge *Based on the book by Irvine Welsh*

## THE GOOD, THE BAD, AND THE UGLY 1966, Italy
**Director:** Sergio Leone
**Cast:** Clint Eastwood, Lee Van Cleef, Eli Wallach
**Screenplay:** Luciano Vincenzoni, Sergio Leone, Agenore Incrocci
and Furio Scarpelli

## AMERICAN BEAUTY 1999, USA
**Director:** Sam Mendes
**Cast:** Kevin Spacey, Annette Bening, Thora Birch
**Screenplay:** Alan Ball

I have existed from the morning of the world and I shall exist until the last star falls from the night. Although I have taken the form of Gaius Caligula, I am all men, as I am no man, and therefore I am a God.

– I realized my true calling in life.
– What's that?
– Shit, man, I'm a natural born killer.

– I'm not gonna debate you, Jerry.
– Okay.
– I'm not gonna sit here and debate.

– I'm not the Messiah! Will you please listen? I am not the Messiah!
Do you understand?! Honestly!
– Only the true Messiah denies His divinity.
– What?! Well, what sort of chance does that give me?
All right! I am the Messiah!
– He is! He is the Messiah!
– Now, fuck off!
– How shall we fuck off, O Lord?

Secret's in the sauce.

I run a couple of newspapers. What do you do?

## CALIGULA 1980, Italy/USA
**Director:** Tinto Brass
**Cast:** Malcolm McDowell, Peter O'Toole, Teresa Ann Savoy
**Screenplay:** Gore Vidal, Bob Guccione, Giancarlo Lui and Franco Rossellini

## NATURAL BORN KILLERS 1994, USA
**Director:** Oliver Stone
**Cast:** Woody Harrelson, Juliette Lewis, Robert Downey Jr.
**Screenplay:** Quentin Tarantino, David Veloz, Richard Rutowski and Oliver Stone

## FARGO 1996, USA
**Director:** Joel Coen  **Cast:** Frances McDormand, William H. Macy, Steve Buscemi
**Screenplay:** Joel Coen and Ethan Coen

## MONTY PYTHON'S LIFE OF BRIAN 1979, United Kingdom
**Director:** Terry Jones
**Cast:** Graham Chapman, John Cleese, Terry Gilliam
**Screenplay:** Graham Chapman, John Cleese, Terry Gilliam, Eric Idle, Terry Jones
and Michael Palin

## FRIED GREEN TOMATOES 1991, USA
**Director:** Jon Avnet
**Cast:** Kathy Bates, Mary-Louise Parker, Mary Stuart Masterson
**Screenplay:** Carol Sobieski, Fannie Flagg *Based on the book by Fannie Flagg*

## CITIZEN KANE 1941, USA
**Director:** Orson Welles
**Cast:** Orson Welles, Joseph Cotten, Everett Sloane
**Screenplay:** Herman J. Mankiewicz and Orson Welles

I think that we can't go around . . . measuring our goodness by what we don't do; by what we deny ourselves, what we resist and who we exclude. I think . . . we've got to measure goodness by what we *embrace*, what we create . . . and who we include.


This here's Miss Bonnie Parker. I'm Clyde Barrow. We rob banks.


–Chief, if I were surrounded by eight or ten of these things, would I stand a chance with them?
–Well, there's no problem. If you have a gun, shoot 'em in the head. That's a sure way to kill 'em. If you don't, get yourself a club or a torch. Beat 'em or burn 'em. They go up pretty easy . . .


Uh-uh, Mother-m-mother, uh, what is the phrase? She isn't quite herself today.


The only evidence I see of the antichrist here, is everyone's desire to see him at work.


You see, before he came down here, it never snowed. And afterwards, it did. If he weren't up there now . . . I don't think it would be snowing. Sometimes you can still catch me dancing in it.

## CHOCOLAT 2000, USA
**Director:** Lasse Hallström
**Cast:** Johnny Depp, Alfred Molina, Lena Olin, Juliette Binoche
**Screenplay:** Robert Nelson Jacobs
*Based on the novel by Joanne Harris*

## BONNIE AND CLYDE 1967, USA
**Director:** Arthur Penn
**Cast:** Warren Beatty, Faye Dunaway, Michael J. Pollard
**Screenplay:** David Newman, Robert Benton and Robert Towne

## NIGHT OF THE LIVING DEAD 1968, USA
**Director:** George A. Romero
**Cast:** Duane Jones, Judith O'Dea, Karl Hardman
**Screenplay:** George A. Romero and John A. Russo

## PSYCHO 1960, USA
**Director:** Alfred Hitchcock
**Cast:** Anthony Perkins, Janet Leigh, Vera Miles
**Screenplay:** Joseph Stefano *Based on the book by Robert Bloch*

## THE NAME OF THE ROSE 1986, France/Italy/West Germany
**Director:** Jean Jacques Annaud
**Cast:** Sean Connery, F. Murray Abraham, Christian Slater
**Screenplay:** Andrew Birkin, Gérard Brach, Howard Franklin and Alain Godard
*Based on the book by Umberto Eco*

## EDWARD SCISSORHANDS 1990, USA
**Director:** Tim Burton
**Cast:** Johnny Depp, Winona Ryder, Dianne Wiest
**Screenplay:** Tim Burton and Caroline Thompson

Let me put it this way, Mr. Amer. The 9000 series is the most reliable computer ever made. No 9000 computer has ever made a mistake or distorted information. We are all, by any practical definition of the words, foolproof and incapable of error.

It's not easy being a cast-iron bitch. It takes discipline, years of training . . . A lot of people don't appreciate that.

–What's your style?
–You can call it the art of fighting without fighting.

Nothing's riding on this except the, uh, first amendment to the Constitution, freedom of the press, and maybe the future of the country. Not that any of that matters, but if you guys fuck up again, I'm going to get mad. Goodnight.

Do you not get it, lads? The Irish are the blacks of Europe. And Dubliners are the blacks of Ireland. And the Northside Dubliners are the blacks of Dublin.  So say it once, say it loud: I'm black and I'm proud.

If you were mine, I wouldn't share you with anybody or anything. It'd be just you and me. We'd be the center of it all. I know it would feel a lot more like love than being left alone with your work.

## 2001: A SPACE ODYSSEY  1968, United Kingdom
**Director:** Stanley Kubrick
**Cast:** Keir Dullea, William Sylvester, Gary Lockwood
**Screenplay:** Stanley Kubrick and Arthur C. Clarke

## THE ABYSS  1989, USA
**Director:** James Cameron
**Cast:** Ed Harris, Mary Elizabeth Mastrantonio, Michael Biehn
**Screenplay:** James Cameron

## ENTER THE DRAGON 1973, USA
**Director:** Robert Clouse  **Cast:** Bruce Lee, John Saxon, Jim Kelly
**Screenplay:** Michael Allin

## ALL THE PRESIDENT'S MEN  1976, USA
**Director:** Alan J. Pakula
**Cast:** Robert Redford, Dustin Hoffman, Jason Robards
**Screenplay:** William Goldman
*Based on the book by Carl Bernstein and Bob Woodward*

## THE COMMITMENTS  1991, Ireland/UK/USA
**Director:** Alan Parker
**Cast:** Robert Arkins, Michael Aherne, Angeline Ball
**Screenplay:** Dick Clement, Ian La Frenais and Roddy Doyle
*Based on the book by Roddy Doyle*

## REDS  1981, USA
**Director:** Warren Beatty  **Cast:** Warren Beatty, Diane Keaton, Edward Herrmann
**Screenplay:** Warren Beatty, Trevor Griffiths, Elaine May, Jeremy Pikser
and Peter S. Feibleman

I just wish for once that you could be in my shoes, Mr. Prosecutor, and then you would know something that you don't know: mercy. That the concept of a society is based on the quality of that mercy; its sense of fair play; its sense of justice! But I guess that's like asking a bear to shit in the toilet.

Afraid this tea is pathetic. I must have used those wretched leaves about twenty times. It's not that I mind so much. Tea without milk is so uncivilized.

Your reality, sir, is lies and balderdash, and I'm delighted to say that I have no grasp of it whatsoever.

The wind whispers of fear and hate. The war has killed love. And those that confess to the Angka are punished, and no one dare ask where they go. Here, only the silent survive.

– If you want me to stop, tell me now.
– No one's asking you to.

– I've just been to the dedication of the new children's park.
– Yeah. How did that go?
– Janice Van Meter got hit with a baseball. It was fabulous.
– Was she hurt?
– I doubt it. She got hit in the head.

## MIDNIGHT EXPRESS 1978, USA
**Director:** Alan Parker
**Cast:** Brad Davis, Irene Miracle, Bo Hopkins
**Screenplay:** Oliver Stone
*Based on the book by Billy Hayes and William Hoffer*

## THE GREAT ESCAPE 1963, USA
**Director:** John Sturges
**Cast:** Steve McQueen, James Garner, Richard Attenborough
**Screenplay:** James Clavell and W.R. Burnett
*Based on the book by Paul Brickhill*

## THE ADVENTURES OF BARON MUNCHAUSEN 1989, United Kingdom
**Director:** Terry Gilliam
**Cast:** John Neville, Eric Idle, Sarah Polley
**Screenplay:** Terry Gilliam and Charles McKeown
*Based on the book by Rudolph Erich Raspe*

## THE KILLING FIELDS 1984, United Kingdom
**Director:** Roland Joffe
**Cast:** Sam Waterston, Haing S. Ngor, John Malkovich
**Screenplay:** Bruce Robinson

## THE BRIDGES OF MADISON COUNTY 1995, USA
**Director:** Clint Eastwood  **Cast:** Clint Eastwood, Meryl Streep, Annie Corley
**Screenplay:** Richard LaGravenese  *Based on the book by Robert James Waller*

## STEEL MAGNOLIAS 1989, USA
**Director:** Herbert Ross
**Cast:** Sally Field, Dolly Parton, Julia Roberts
**Screenplay:** Robert Harling

– But Mama, the men she finds. The last one was so
old and he was bald. He had no hair.
– A poor girl without a dowry can't be so particular.
You want hair, marry a monkey.

You know something? You read too many comic books.

Oh, this young man has had a very trying rookie season, with the
litigation, the notoriety, his subsequent deportation to Canada and
that country's refusal to accept him, well, I guess that's more than
most 21-year-olds can handle. Number six, Ogie Oglethorpe.

– There are two ways to disable a croc, you know.
– I don't suppose you'd care to tell me what they are.
– One way is to take a pencil and stick
it in the pressure area above it's eye.
– And the other way?
– Oh, the other way is twice as simple. Just stick your
hand in its mouth and pull its teeth out. Heh, heh.

Well I wouldn't kick Mick Jagger out of my bed,
but, uh, I'm not a homosexual, no.

## FIDDLER ON THE ROOF 1971, USA
**Director:** Norman Jewison
**Cast:** (Chaim) Topol, Norma Crane, Leonard Frey
**Screenplay:** Joseph Stein
*Based on the book by Sholom Aleichem*

## REBEL WITHOUT A CAUSE 1955, USA
**Director:** Nicholas Ray
**Cast:** James Dean, Natalie Wood, Sal Mineo
**Screenplay:** Nicholas Ray, Irving Shulman and Stewart Stern

## SLAP SHOT 1977, USA
**Director:** George Roy Hill
**Cast:** Paul Newman, Michael Ontkean, Lindsay Crouse
**Screenplay:** Nancy Dowd

## LIVE AND LET DIE 1973, United Kingdom
**Director:** Guy Hamilton
**Cast:** Roger Moore, Yaphet Kotto, Jane Seymour
**Screenplay:** Tom Mankiewicz
*Based on the book by Ian Fleming*

## HAIR 1979, USA
**Director:** Milos Forman
**Cast:** John Savage, Treat Williams, Beverly D'Angelo
**Screenplay:** Gerome Ragni, James Rado, and Michael Weller

– Maybe you shouldn't drink so much.
– Maybe I shouldn't breathe so much either.


– His high exaltedness, the Great Jabba the Hutt,
has decreed that you are to be terminated immediately.
– Good, I hate long waits.


You can turn your back on a person, but don't ever turn your
back on a drug. Especially when it's waving a razor-sharp hunting
knife in your eye.


Men would pay $200 for me, and here you are turning down
a freebie. You could get a perfectly good dishwasher for that.


– Have you ever seen a Commie drink a glass of water?
– Well, I can't say I have.


A lot of holes in the desert, and a lot of problems are buried in
those holes. But you gotta do it right. I mean, you gotta have the
hole already dug before you show up with a package in the trunk.
Otherwise, you're talking about a half-hour to forty-five minutes
worth of digging. And who knows who's gonna come along in
that time? Pretty soon, you gotta dig a few more holes.
You could be there all fuckin' night.

## LEAVING LAS VEGAS 1995, USA
**Director:** Mike Figgis
**Cast:** Nicolas Cage, Elisabeth Shue, Julian Sands
**Screenplay:** Mike Figgis *Based on the book by John O'Brien*

## RETURN OF THE JEDI 1983, USA
**Director:** Richard Marquand
**Cast:** Mark Hamill, Harrison Ford, Carrie Fisher
**Screenplay:** George Lucas and Lawrence Kasdan

## FEAR AND LOATHING IN LAS VEGAS 1998, USA
**Director:** Terry Gilliam
**Cast:** Johnny Depp, Benicio Del Toro, Tobey Maguire
**Screenplay:** Terry Gilliam, Tony Grisoni, Tod Davies and Alex Cox
*Based on the book by Hunter S. Thompson*

## KLUTE 1971, USA
**Director:** Alan J. Pakula **Cast:** Jane Fonda, Donald Sutherland, Charles Cioffi
**Screenplay:** Andy Lewis and Dave Lewis

## DR. STRANGELOVE OR: HOW I LEARNED TO STOP WORRYING AND LOVE THE BOMB 1964, USA
**Director:** Stanley Kubrick **Cast:** Peter Sellers, George C. Scott, Sterling Hayden
**Screenplay:** Stanley Kubrick, Terry Southern and Peter George
*Based on the book by Peter George*

## CASINO 1995, USA
**Director:** Martin Scorsese
**Cast:** Robert De Niro, Sharon Stone, Joe Pesci
**Screenplay:** Nicholas Pileggi and Martin Scorsese
*Based on the book by Nicholas Pileggi*

Courage! What makes a king out of a slave? What makes the flag on the mast to wave? Courage. What makes the elephant charge his tusk in the misty mist, or the dusky dusk? What makes the muskrat guard his musk? Courage. What makes the sphinx the seventh wonder? Courage. What makes the dawn come up like thunder? Courage. What makes the Hottentot so hot? What puts the ape in apricot? What have they got that I ain't got?
– Courage!

I don't make things difficult. That's the way they get, all by themselves.

– You're late.
– You're stunning.
– You're forgiven.

I could have killed 'em all! I could kill you. In town, you're the law; out here it's me. Don't push it. Don't push it or I'll give you a war you won't believe. Let it go. Let it go.

I thought you knew! I want to go through life jumping into fountains naked, good night!

Bring the dog: I love animals . . . I'm a great cook.

## THE WIZARD OF OZ  1939, USA
**Director:** Victor Fleming
**Cast:** Judy Garland, Ray Bolger, Bert Lahr
**Screenplay:** Noel Langley, Florence Ryerson and Edgar Allan Woolf
*Based on the book by L. Frank Baum*

## LETHAL WEAPON  1987, USA
**Director:** Richard Donner  **Cast:** Mel Gibson, Danny Glover, Gary Busey
**Screenplay:** Shane Black

## PRETTY WOMAN  1990, USA
**Director:** Garry Marshall
**Cast:** Richard Gere, Julia Roberts, Ralph Bellamy
**Screenplay:** J.F. Lawton

## FIRST BLOOD  1982, USA
**Director:** Ted Kotcheff
**Cast:** Sylvester Stallone, Richard Crenna, Brian Dennehy
**Screenplay:** Michael Kozoll, William Sackheim and Sylvester Stallone
*Based on the book by David Morrell*

## THE BIRDS  1963, USA
**Director:** Alfred Hitchcock
**Cast:** Rod Taylor, Tippi Hedren, Jessica Tandy
**Screenplay:** Daphne Du Maurier and Evan Hunter

## FATAL ATTRACTION  1987, USA
**Director:** Adrian Lyne
**Cast:** Michael Douglas, Glenn Close, Anne Archer
**Screenplay:** James Dearden and Nicholas Meyer

–Well, I think I'll get saddled up and go looking for a woman.
–Good hunting.
–Shouldn't take more than a couple of days. I'm not picky. As long as she's smart, pretty, and sweet, and gentle, and tender, and refined, and lovely, and carefree . . .


I just want to apologize to Josh's mom, and Mike's mom, and my mom. I am so sorry! Because it was my fault. I was the one who brought them here. I was the one that said keep going south. I was the one who said that we were not lost. It was my fault, because it was my project. I am so scared! I don't know what's out there. We are going to die out here! I am so scared!

Life all comes down to a few moments. This is one of them.


A relationship, I think, is like a shark. You know? It has to constantly move forward or it dies. And I think what we got on our hands is a dead shark.


Real diamonds! They must be worth their weight in gold!


The son of a bitch is here. I saw him. I'm gonna get him.

## BUTCH CASSIDY AND THE SUNDANCE KID 1969, USA
**Director:** George Roy Hill
**Cast:** Paul Newman, Robert Redford, Katharine Ross
**Screenplay:** William Goldman


## THE BLAIR WITCH PROJECT 1999, USA
**Director:** Daniel Myrick, Eduardo Sánchez
**Cast:** Heather Donahue, Joshua Leonard, Michael C. Williams
**Screenplay:** Daniel Myrick and Eduardo Sánchez


## WALL STREET 1987, USA
**Director:** Oliver Stone
**Cast:** Michael Douglas, Charlie Sheen, Daryl Hannah
**Screenplay:** Stanley Weiser and Oliver Stone

## ANNIE HALL 1977, USA
**Director:** Woody Allen
**Cast:** Woody Allen, Diane Keaton, Tony Roberts
**Screenplay:** Woody Allen and Marshall Brickman

## SOME LIKE IT HOT 1959, USA
**Director:** Billy Wilder
**Cast:** Jack Lemmon, Tony Curtis, Marilyn Monroe
**Screenplay:** Robert Thoeren, M. Logan, Billy Wilder and I.A.L. Diamond

## THE FRENCH CONNECTION 1971, USA
**Director:** William Friedkin  **Cast:** Gene Hackman, Fernando Rey, Roy Scheider
**Screenplay:** Ernest Tidyman and Edward M. Keyes
*Based on the book by Robin Moore*

– Say Lou, didya hear the one about the guy who couldn't afford
personalized plate so he went and changed his name to J3L2404?
– Yah, that's a good one.

You see, Danny, I can deal with the bullets, and the bombs, and the
blood. I don't want money, and I don't want medals. What I do want is
for you to stand there in that faggoty white uniform and with your
Harvard mouth extend me some fucking courtesy. You gotta ask me nicely.

– What the hell you wanna go mess around that river for?
– Because it's there.
– It's there alright and you get in it and
can't git out, you gonna wish it wasn't.

– Sixty years old and still getting crushes on other men's wives.
I would hope by the time I'm your age, I'm a little smarter than that.
– Can't hurt to hope. You sure are off to a slow start.

The only thing we had in common was that she was from Iowa,
and I had once heard of Iowa.

## FARGO  1996, USA
**Director:** Joel Coen
**Cast:** Frances McDormand, William H. Macy, Steve Buscemi
**Screenplay:** Joel Coen and Ethan Coen

## A FEW GOOD MEN  1992, USA
**Director:** Rob Reiner
**Cast:** Tom Cruise, Jack Nicholson, Demi Moore
**Screenplay:** Aaron Sorkin

## DELIVERANCE  1972, USA
**Director:** John Boorman
**Cast:** Jon Voight, Burt Reynolds, Ned Beatty
**Screenplay:** James Dickey
*Based on the book by James Dickey*

## NOBODY'S FOOL  1994, USA
**Director:** Robert Benton
**Cast:** Paul Newman, Jessica Tandy, Bruce Willis
**Screenplay:** Robert Benton
*Based on the book by Richard Russo*

## FIELD OF DREAMS  1989, USA
**Director:** Phil Alden Robinson
**Cast:** Kevin Costner, Amy Madigan, Gaby Hoffmann
**Screenplay:** Phil Alden Robinson
*Based on the book W.P. Kinsella*

I don't believe that God made man in his image. 'Cause most of the shit that happens comes from man. Now, I think man was made in the Devil's image, and women were created out of God's. 'Cause after all, women can have babies, which is kind of like creating. And which also counts for the fact that women are so attracted to men . . . 'cause let's face it . . . the Devil is a hell of a lot more interesting! So the whole point in life is for men and women to get married . . . so that God and the Devil can get together and work it out.

I'll make him an offer he can't refuse.

You're a big man, but you're out of shape.
With me it's a full time job. Now behave yourself.

I'm a connoisseur of roads. I've been tasting roads
my whole life. This road will never end. It probably goes
all around the world.

I was murdered, an unnatural death, and now I walk
the earth in limbo until the werewolf's curse is lifted.

I should've given you to God when you were born,
but I was weak and backsliding . . .

## THE FISHER KING 1991, USA
**Director:** Terry Gilliam
**Cast:** Robin Williams, Jeff Bridges, Amanda Plummer
**Screenplay:** Richard LaGravenese

## THE GODFATHER 1972, USA
**Director:** Francis Ford Coppola
**Cast:** Marlon Brando, Al Pacino, James Caan
**Screenplay:** Mario Puzo and Francis Ford Coppola *Based on the book by Mario Puzo*

## GET CARTER 1971, United Kingdom
**Director:** Mike Hodges
**Cast:** Michael Caine, Ian Hendry, Britt Ekland
**Screenplay:** Mike Hodges *Based on the book by Ted Lewis (III)*

## MY OWN PRIVATE IDAHO 1991, USA
**Director:** Gus Van Sant
**Cast:** River Phoenix, Keanu Reeves, James Russo
**Screenplay:** Gus Van Sant

## AN AMERICAN WEREWOLF IN LONDON 1981, USA
**Director:** John Landis
**Cast:** David Naughton, Jenny Agutter, Griffin Dunne
**Screenplay:** John Landis

## CARRIE 1976, USA
**Director:** Brian De Palma
**Cast:** Sissy Spacek, Piper Laurie, William Katt
**Screenplay:** Lawrence D. Cohen *Based on the book by Stephen King*

Don't worry! As long as you hit that wire with the connecting hook at precisely eighty-eight miles per hour the instant the lightning strikes the tower ... everything will be fine!

They was giving me ten thousand watts a day, you know, and I'm hot to trot! The next woman takes me on's gonna light up like a pinball machine and pay off in silver dollars!

The 70s are dead and gone. The 80s are going to be something wonderfully new and different, and so am I.

The light that burns twice as bright burns for half as long and you have burned so very, very brightly, Roy.

I think you should send us the biggest transport plane you have, and take this thing to the Arctic or somewhere and drop it where it will never thaw.

Soul is the music people understand. Sure it's basic and it's simple, but it's something else 'cause, 'cause, 'cause it's honest. That's it. It's honest. There's no fuckin' bullshit. It sticks its neck out and says it straight from the heart. Sure there's a lot of different music you can get off on but soul is more than that. It takes you somewhere else. It grabs you by the balls and lifts you above the shite.

## BACK TO THE FUTURE   1985, USA
**Director:** Robert Zemeckis
**Cast:** Michael J. Fox, Christopher Lloyd, Crispin Glover
**Screenplay:** Robert Zemeckis and Bob Gale

## ONE FLEW OVER THE CUCKOO'S NEST 1975, USA
**Director:** Milos Forman
**Cast:** Jack Nicholson, Louise Fletcher, Brad Dourif
**Screenplay:** Bo Goldman and Lawrence Hauben
*Based on the book by Ken Kesey*

## CAN'T STOP THE MUSIC   1980, USA
**Director:** Nancy Walker
**Cast:** Alex Briley, David Hodo, Glenn Hughes
**Screenplay:** Alan Carr and Bronte Woodard

## BLADE RUNNER   1982, USA
**Director:** Ridley Scott
**Cast:** Harrison Ford, Rutger Hauer, Sean Young
**Screenplay:** Hampton Fancher, David Webb Peoples, Roland Kibbee
*Based on the book by Philip K. Dick*

## THE BLOB   1958, USA
**Director:** Irwin S. Yeaworth Jr.
**Cast:** Steve McQueen, Aneta Corsaut, Earl Rowe
**Screenplay:** Kay Linaker and Irvine H. Millgate

## THE COMMITMENTS   1991, Ireland/UK/USA
**Director:** Alan Parker
**Cast:** Robert Arkins, Michael Aherne, Angeline Ball
**Screenplay:** Dick Clement, Ian La Frenais and Roddy Doyle
*Based on the book by Roddy Doyle*

All of you! You all killed him! And my brother, and Riff.
Not with bullets, or guns. With hate. Well, now I can kill,
too, because now I have hate!

There's nothing more irresistible to a man than a woman
who's in love with him.

For a nation of pigs, it sures seems funny that you don't eat them!
Jesus Christ forgave the bastards, but I can't! I hate! I hate you! I hate
your nation! And I hate your people! And I fuck your sons and
daughters because they're pigs! You're all pigs!

Geology is the study of pressure and time. Thats all it takes,
really. Pressure . . . and time. That, and a big goddamn poster.

I'd say the odds against a successful escape are about 100 to
one. But may I add another word, Colonel? The odds against
survival in this camp are even worse.

Loneliness has followed me my whole life. Everywhere.
In bars, in cars, sidewalks, stores, everywhere. There's
no escape. I'm God's lonely man.

## WEST SIDE STORY 1961, USA
**Director:** Robert Wise, Jerome Robbins
**Cast:** Natalie Wood, Richard Beymer, George Chakiris
**Screenplay:** Jerome Robbins, Arthur Laurents and Ernest Lehman
*Based on the play* Romeo and Juliet *by William Shakespeare*

## THE SOUND OF MUSIC 1965, USA
**Director:** Robert Wise
**Cast:** Julie Andrews, Christopher Plummer, Eleanor Parker
**Screenplay:** Ernest Lehman
*Based on the book by Howard Lindsay and Russel Crouse*

## MIDNIGHT EXPRESS 1978, USA
**Director:** Alan Parker
**Cast:** Brad Davis, Irene Miracle, Bo Hopkins
**Screenplay:** Oliver Stone
*Based on the book by Billy Hayes and William Hoffer*

## THE SHAWSHANK REDEMPTION 1994, USA
**Director:** Frank Darabont
**Cast:** Tim Robbins, Morgan Freeman, Bob Gunton
**Screenplay:** Frank Darabont
*Based on the book by Stephen King*

## THE BRIDGE ON THE RIVER KWAI 1957, United Kingdom
**Director:** David Lean
**Cast:** William Holden, Alec Guinness, Jack Hawkins
**Screenplay:** Michael Wilson, Carl Foreman *Based on the book by Pierre Boulle*

## TAXI DRIVER 1976, USA
**Director:** Martin Scorsese
**Cast:** Robert De Niro, Cybill Shepherd, Harvey Keitel
**Screenplay:** Paul Schrader

. . . I'm sure it comes as no great suprise to you when I say that there are little corners in everyone which were better off left alone; sicknesses, weaknesses, which should never be exposed. But . . . that's your stock in trade, isn't it—a man's weakness? And I was never really fully aware of mine . . . Until you brought them out.

We'll make a great team, old man. You for the words, me for the pictures. I can be your eyes.

You wanna see dry land. You really wanna see it? I'll take you there.

We must be like the ox, and have no thought, except for the Party. And have no love, but for the Angka. People starve, but we must not grow food. We must honor the comrade children, whose minds are not corrupted by the past.

. . . It ain't so easy to shoot a man anyhow, especially if the son-of-a-bitch is shootin' back at you.

We all dream of being a child again, even the worst of us. Perhaps the worst most of all.

## KLUTE 1971, USA
**Director:** Alan J. Pakula
**Cast:** Jane Fonda, Donald Sutherland, Charles Cioffi
**Screenplay:** Andy Lewis and Dave Lewis

## THE YEAR OF LIVING DANGEROUSLY 1982, Australia
**Director:** Peter Weir
**Cast:** Mel Gibson, Linda Hunt, Sigourney Weaver
**Screenplay:** C.J. Koch, Peter Weir and David Williamson
*Based on the book by C.J. Koch*

## WATERWORLD 1995, USA
**Director:** Kevin Reynolds
**Cast:** Kevin Costner, Dennis Hopper, Jeanne Tripplehorn
**Screenplay:** Peter Rader and David Twohy

## THE KILLING FIELDS 1984, United Kingdom
**Director:** Roland Joffe
**Cast:** Sam Waterston, Haing S. Ngor, John Malkovich
**Screenplay:** Bruce Robinson

## UNFORGIVEN 1992, USA
**Director:** Clint Eastwood
**Cast:** Clint Eastwood, Gene Hackman, Morgan Freeman
**Screenplay:** David Webb Peoples

## THE WILD BUNCH 1969, USA
**Director:** Sam Peckinpah
**Cast:** William Holden, Ernest Borgnine, Robert Ryan
**Screenplay:** Walon Green and Sam Peckinpah

Would ya just watch the hair. Ya know, I work on my
hair a long time and you hit it. He hits my hair.

– Who are you?
– Some call me one thing and some another.
– What do they call you the most?
– By my name. Cherry Valance.

I have no plans to call on you, Clarice.
The world is more interesting with you in it.

– I'm not a fool, Plissken!
– Call me Snake.

You've got to remember that these are just simple farmers.
These are people of the land. The common clay of the new West.
You know . . . morons.

## SATURDAY NIGHT FEVER  1977, USA
**Director:** John Badham
**Cast:** John Travolta, Karen Lynn Gorney, Barry Miller
**Screenplay:** Nik Cohn and Norman Wexler

## RED RIVER  1948, USA
**Director:** Howard Hawks
**Cast:** John Wayne, Montgomery Clift, Walter Brennan
**Screenplay:** Borden Chase and Charles Schnee

## THE SILENCE OF THE LAMBS  1991, USA
**Director:** Jonathan Demme
**Cast:** Jodie Foster, Anthony Hopkins, Scott Glenn
**Screenplay:** Ted Tally
*Based on the book by Thomas Harris*

## ESCAPE FROM NEW YORK  1981, USA
**Director:** John Carpenter
**Cast:** Kurt Russell, Lee Van Cleef, Ernest Borgnine
**Screenplay:** John Carpenter and Nick Castle

## BLAZING SADDLES  1974, USA
**Director:** Mel Brooks
**Cast:** Cleavon Little, Gene Wilder, Harvey Korman
**Screenplay:** Andrew Bergman, Mel Brooks, Richard Pryor, Norman Steinberg
    and Alan Uger

– Nervous?

– Yes.

– First time?

– No, I've been nervous lots of times.

– There are ways of telling whether she is a witch.

– Are there? Oh well, tell us!

– Tell me. What do you do with witches?

– Burn them!

– And what do you burn, apart from witches?

– More witches!

– Wood!

– Now, why do witches burn?

– . . . because they're made of . . . wood?

– Good. So how do you tell whether she is made of wood?

– Build a bridge out of her!

– But don't we also build bridges out of stone?

– Oh yeah. . . .

That's more than a dress. That's an Audrey Hepburn movie.

I tried to capture the spirit of the thing.

Up in the sky, look! It's a bird! It's a plane!

## AIRPLANE! / FLYING HIGH 1980, USA
**Director:** Jim Abrahams, David Zucker, Jerry Zucker
**Cast:** Robert Hays, Julie Hagerty, Robert Stack
**Screenplay:** Jim Abrahams, David Zucker and Jerry Zucker

## MONTY PYTHON AND THE HOLY GRAIL 1975, United Kingdom
**Director:** Terry Gilliam, Terry Jones
**Cast:** Graham Chapman, John Cleese, Terry Gilliam
**Screenplay:** Graham Chapman, John Cleese, Eric Idle, Terry Gilliam, Terry Jones and Michael Palin

## JERRY MAGUIRE 1996, USA
**Director:** Cameron Crowe
**Cast:** Tom Cruise, Cuba Gooding Jr., Renee Zellweger
**Screenplay:** Cameron Crowe

## SLAP SHOT 1977, USA
**Director:** George Roy Hill
**Cast:** Paul Newman, Michael Ontkean, Lindsay Crouse
**Screenplay:** Nancy Dowd

## SUPERMAN 1941, USA
**Director:** Dave Fleischer
**Cast:** Bud Collyer (voice), Joan Alexander (voice)
**Screenplay:** Seymour Kneitel and Joe Shuster

– Isn't that your phone number?
– Is it? I don't call myself that often.

That's incredible. Imagine seven million people all wanting to live together. Yeah, New York must be the friendliest place on earth.

– You must have shot an awful lot of tigers, Sir.
– Yes, I used a machine-gun.

– Apparently the only performance that will satisfy you is when I play dead.
– Your very next role, and you'll be quite convincing, I assure you.

– He's just doing it to get a rise out of you. Just ignore him.
– Sweets, you couldn't ignore me if you tried.
– So . . . so. Are you guys like boyfriend-girlfriend? Steady dates? Lovers? Come on, Sporto, level with me. Do you slip her the hot beef injection?

The rest is silence.

## CHINATOWN 1974, USA
**Director:** Roman Polanski
**Cast:** Jack Nicholson, Faye Dunaway, John Huston
**Screenplay:** Robert Towne and Roman Polanski

## CROCODILE DUNDEE 1986, Australia
**Director:** Peter Faiman
**Cast:** Paul Hogan, Linda Kozlowski, John Meillon
**Screenplay:** John Cornell, Paul Hogan and Ken Shadie

## THE ITALIAN JOB 1969, United Kingdom
**Director:** Peter Collinson
**Cast:** Michael Caine, Noel Coward, Maggie Blye
**Screenplay:** Troy Kennedy-Martin

## NORTH BY NORTHWEST 1959, USA
**Director:** Alfred Hitchcock
**Cast:** Cary Grant, Eva Marie Saint, James Mason
**Screenplay:** Ernest Lehman

## THE BREAKFAST CLUB 1985, USA
**Director:** John Hughes
**Cast:** Emilio Estevez, Judd Nelson, Molly Ringwald
**Screenplay:** John Hughes

## HAIR 1979, USA
**Director:** Milos Forman
**Cast:** John Savage, Treat Williams, Beverly D'Angelo
**Screenplay:** Gerome Ragni, James Rado, Galt MacDermot and Michael Weller

A fellow will remember a lot of things you wouldn't think he'd remember. You take me. One day, back in 1896, I was crossing over to Jersey on the ferry, and as we pulled out, there was another ferry pulling in, and on it there was a girl waiting to get off. A white dress she had on. She was carrying a white parasol. I only saw her for one second. She didn't see me at all, but I'll bet a month hasn't gone by since that I haven't thought of that girl.

– Why don't you kiss her instead of talking her to death?
– You want me to kiss her, huh?
– Ah, youth is wasted on the wrong people!

What a fitting end to your life's pursuits. You're about to become a permanent addition to this archaeological find. Who knows? In a thousand years, even you may be worth something.

Yippee-ki-yay, motherfucker!

Look spaghetti arms. This is my dance space. This is your dance space. I don't go into yours, you don't go into mine. You gotta hold the frame.

We were all feeling a bit shagged and fagged and fashed, it being a night of no small expenditure.

## CITIZEN KANE 1941, USA
**Director:** Orson Welles
**Cast:** Orson Welles, Joseph Cotten, Everett Sloane
**Screenplay:** Herman J. Mankiewicz and Orson Welles

## IT'S A WONDERFUL LIFE 1946, USA
**Director:** Frank Capra
**Cast:** James Stewart, Donna Reed, Lionel Barrymore
**Screenplay:** Philip Van Doren Stern, Frances Goodrich, Albert Hackett, Frank Capra, Jo Swerling and Michael Wilson

## RAIDERS OF THE LOST ARK 1981, USA
**Director:** Steven Spielberg
**Cast:** Harrison Ford, Karen Allen, Wolf Kahler
**Screenplay:** George Lucas, Philip Kaufman and Lawrence Kasdan

## DIE HARD 1988, USA
**Director:** John McTiernan
**Cast:** Bruce Willis, Alan Rickman, Bonnie Bedelia
**Screenplay:** Jeb Stuart and Steven E. de Souza
*Based on the book by Roderick Thorp*

## DIRTY DANCING 1987, USA
**Director:** Emile Ardolino
**Cast:** Jennifer Grey, Patrick Swayze, Jerry Orbach
**Screenplay:** Eleanor Bergstein

## A CLOCKWORK ORANGE 1971, USA
**Director:** Stanley Kubrick
**Cast:** Malcolm McDowell, Patrick Magee, Adrienne Corri
**Screenplay:** Stanley Kubrick *Based on the book by Anthony Burgess*

Cargo and ship destroyed. I should reach the frontier in about six weeks. With a little luck, the network will pick me up. This is Ripley, last survivor of the Nostromo, signing off.

Antony is dead? You say that as if it were a everyday occurence. The soup is hot, the soup is cold. Antony is alive, Antony is dead.

Well, what am I supposed to do? You won't answers my calls. You change your number. I mean, I'm not gonna be ignored, Dan!

I don't have to take this abuse from you. I've got hundreds of people dying to abuse me.

And, you know, the thing about a shark . . . he's got lifeless eyes. Black eyes. Like a doll's eyes. When he comes at ya, doesn't seem to be living . . . until he bites ya, and those black eyes roll over white.

– How's east?
– East?
– Yeah, we've been going south all this time. How's east?
– Wicked Witch of the West, Wicked Witch of the East. Which one was bad?
– Wicked Witch of the West was the bad one.
– Then we should go east.

## ALIEN 1979, USA
**Director:** Ridley Scott **Cast:** Tom Skerritt, Sigourney Weaver, John Hurt
**Screenplay:** Dan O'Bannon, Ronald Shusett and Dan O'Bannon


## CLEOPATRA 1963, USA
**Director:** Joseph L. Mankiewicz
**Cast:** Elizabeth Taylor, Richard Burton, Rex Harrison
**Screenplay:** Sidney Buchman, Ben Hecht, Ranald MacDougall and
Joseph L. Mankiewicz *Based on the book by Carlo Mario Franzero*

## FATAL ATTRACTION 1987, USA
**Director:** Adrian Lyne **Cast:** Michael Douglas, Glenn Close, Anne Archer
**Screenplay:** James Dearden and Nicholas Meyer

## GHOSTBUSTERS 1984, USA
**Director:** Ivan Reitman
**Cast:** Bill Murray, Dan Aykroyd, Harold Ramis
**Screenplay:** Dan Aykroyd, Harold Ramis and Rick Moranis

## JAWS 1975, USA
**Director:** Steven Spielberg
**Cast:** Roy Scheider, Robert Shaw, Richard Dreyfuss
**Screenplay:** Peter Benchley, Carl Gottlieb, John Milius, Howard Sackler
and Robert Shaw *Based on the book by Peter Benchley*

## THE BLAIR WITCH PROJECT 1999, USA
**Director:** Daniel Myrick, Eduardo Sánchez
**Cast:** Heather Donahue, Joshua Leonard, Michael C. Williams
**Screenplay:** Daniel Myrick and Eduardo Sánchez

Gareth used to prefer funerals to weddings. He said it was easier to get enthusiastic about a ceremony one had an outside chance of eventually being involved in.

– Oh, waiter!
– That is not a waiter, my dear. That is a butler.
– Well, I can't yell Oh, butler! can I?
Maybe somebody's name is Butler.
– You have a point. An idiotic one, but a point.

– It's so clean out here!
– That's because they don't throw their garbage away. They turn it into television shows.

I'm afraid I'm gonna have to pull rank on you. I didn't want to have do this. I'm with the Mattress Police. There are no tags on these mattresses.

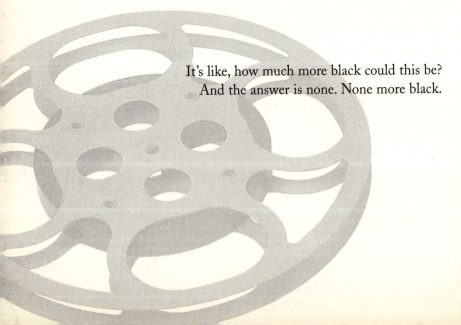

It's like, how much more black could this be? And the answer is none. None more black.

## FOUR WEDDINGS AND A FUNERAL 1994, United Kingdom
**Director:** Mike Newell
**Cast:** Hugh Grant, Andie MacDowell, Kristin Scott Thomas
**Screenplay:** Richard Curtis

## ALL ABOUT EVE 1950, USA
**Director:** Joseph L. Mankiewicz
**Cast:** Bette Davis, Anne Baxter, George Sanders
**Screenplay:** Joseph L. Mankiewicz and Mary Orr

## ANNIE HALL 1977, USA
**Director:** Woody Allen
**Cast:** Woody Allen, Diane Keaton, Tony Roberts
**Screenplay:** Woody Allen and Marshall Brickman

## FLETCH 1985, USA
**Director:** Michael Ritchie
**Cast:** Chevy Chase, Dana Wheeler Nicholson, Tim Matheson
**Screenplay:** Andrew Bergman
*Based on the book by Gregory McDonald*

## THIS IS SPINAL TAP 1984, USA
**Director:** Rob Reiner
**Cast:** Michael McKean, Christopher Guest, Harry Shearer
**Screenplay:** Christopher Guest, Michael McKean, Rob Reiner and Harry Shearer

I know what you're thinking. Did he fire six shots or only five? Well, to tell you the truth, in all this excitement, I've kinda lost track myself. But, being as this is a .44 Magnum, the most powerful handgun in the world, and would blow your head clean off, you've got to ask yourself one question: Do I feel lucky? Well, do ya punk?

. . . You never really understand a person until you consider things from his point of view: until you climb inside of his skin and walk around in it.

– You want answers?
– I think I'm entitled.
– You want answers?
– I want the truth!
– You can't handle the truth!

Your eyes are full of hate, forty-one. That's good. Hate keeps a man alive.

Nobody puts baby in a corner.

## DIRTY HARRY  1971, USA
**Director:** Don Siegal
**Cast:** Clint Eastwood, Harry Guardino, Reni Santoni
**Screenplay:** Harry Julian Fink, Rita M. Fink, Dean Riesner and John Milius

## TO KILL A MOCKINGBIRD  1962, USA
**Director:** Robert Mulligan
**Cast:** Gregory Peck, Mary Badham, Philip Alford
**Screenplay:** Horton Foote
*Based on the book by Harper Lee*

## A FEW GOOD MEN  1992, USA
**Director:** Rob Reiner
**Cast:** Tom Cruise, Jack Nicholson, Demi Moore
**Screenplay:** Aaron Sorkin

## BEN-HUR  1959, USA
**Director:** William Wyler
**Cast:** Charlton Heston, Jack Hawkins, Stephen Boyd
**Screenplay:** Karl Tunberg, Maxwell Anderson, Christopher Fry and Gore Vidal
*Based on the book by Lew Wallace*

## DIRTY DANCING  1987, USA
**Director:** Emile Ardolino
**Cast:** Jennifer Grey, Patrick Swayze, Jerry Orbach
**Screenplay:** Eleanor Bergstein

Don't you think I realize what's going on here, Miss? Who do you think I am, huh? Don't you think I know that if I was some hotshot from out of town that pulled inside here and you guys made a reservation mistake, I'd be the first one to get a room and I'd be upstairs relaxing right now? But I'm not some hotshot from out of town. I'm a small reporter from Rolling Stone magazine that's in town to do an exclusive interview with Michael Jackson that's gonna be picked up by every major magazine in the country. I was gonna call the article Michael Jackson Is Sitting On Top of the World, but now I think I might as well just call it Michael Jackson Can Sit On Top of the World Just As Long As He Doesn't Sit in the Beverly Palm Hotel 'Cause There's No Niggers Allowed in There!

The whole thing stinks like yesterday's diapers!

I can't lie to you about your chances, but . . . you have my sympathies.

A heart can be broken, but it will keep beating just the same.

Come on, now. Don't be naive, Lieutenant. We both know how careers are made. Integrity is something you sell the public.

Let them hate me. So long as they fear me!

## BEVERLY HILLS COP 1984, USA
**Director:** Martin Brest
**Cast:** Eddie Murphy, Judge Reinhold, John Ashton
**Screenplay:** Danilo Bach and Daniel Petrie Jr.

## WHO FRAMED ROGER RABBIT 1988, USA
**Director:** Robert Zemeckis **Cast:** Bob Hoskins, Christopher Lloyd, Joanna Cassidy
**Screenplay:** Jeffrey Price and Peter S. Seaman *Based on the book by Gary K. Wolf*

## ALIEN 1979, USA
**Director:** Ridley Scott **Cast:** Tom Skerritt, Sigourney Weaver, John Hurt
**Screenplay:** Dan O'Bannon, Ronald Shusett, Dan O'Bannon, David Giler and Walter Hill

## FRIED GREEN TOMATOES 1991, USA
**Director:** Jon Avnet **Cast:** Kathy Bates, Mary-Louise-Parker, Mary Stuart Masterson
**Screenplay:** Carol Sobieski, Fannie Flagg
*Based on the book by Fannie Flagg*

## BULLITT 1968, USA
**Director:** Peter Yates **Cast:** Steve McQueen, Robert Vaughn, Jacqueline Bisset
**Screenplay:** Alan Trustman and Harry Kleiner *Based on the book by Robert L. Pike*

## CALIGULA 1980, Italy/USA
**Director:** Tinto Brass **Cast:** Malcolm McDowell, Peter O'Toole, Teresa Ann Savoy
**Screenplay:** Gore Vidal, Bob Guccione, Giancarlo Lui and Franco Rossellini

– Whose motorcycle is this?
– It's a chopper, baby.
– Whose chopper is this?
– It's Zed's.
– Who's Zed?
– Zed's dead, baby. Zed's dead.

It's a Sicilian message.
It means Luca Brasi sleeps with the fishes.

Every day above ground is a good day.

Now take that underwear off your head. Enough's enough.

Rockin' good news.

## PULP FICTION 1994, USA
**Director:** Quentin Tarantino
**Cast:** John Travolta, Samuel L. Jackson, Uma Thurman
**Screenplay:** Quentin Tarantino and Roger Avary

## THE GODFATHER 1972, USA
**Director:** Francis Ford Coppola
**Cast:** Marlon Brando, Al Pacino, James Caan
**Screenplay:** Mario Puzo and Francis Ford Coppola *Based on the book by Mario Puzo*

## SCARFACE 1983, USA
**Director:** Brian De Palma
**Cast:** Al Pacino, Steven Bauer, Michelle Pfeiffer
**Screenplay:** Oliver Stone and Howard Hawks *Based on the book by Armitage Trail*

## KELLY'S HEROES 1970, USA
**Director:** Brian G. Hutton
**Cast:** Clint Eastwood, Telly Savalas, Don Rickles
**Screenplay:** Troy Kennedy-Martin

## WILD AT HEART 1990, USA
**Director:** David Lynch
**Cast:** Nicolas Cage, Laura Dern, Diane Ladd
**Screenplay:** David Lynch
*Based on the book by Barry Gifford*

– What's forget about it?

– Forget about it is like if you agree with someone, you know, like Raquel Welch is one great piece of ass, forget about it. But then, if you disagree, like a Lincoln is better than a Cadillac? Forget about it! You know? But then, it's also like if something's the greatest thing in the world, like mingia those peppers, forget about it. But it's also like saying Go to hell! too. Like, you know, like Hey Paulie, you got a one inch pecker? and Paulie says Forget about it! Sometimes it just means forget about it.

– Have you no fear, English?
– My fear is my concern.

I will not be threatened by a walking meat loaf!

I know now that my wife has become host to a Candarian demon. I fear that the only way to stop those possessed by the spirits of the book is through the act of . . . bodily dismemberment.

Do you know what she did, your cunting daughter?

I just can't take no pleasure in killing. There's just some things you gotta do. Don't mean you have to like it.

## DONNIE BRASCO 1997, USA
**Director:** Mike Newell
**Cast:** Al Pacino, Johnny Depp, Michael Madsen
**Screenplay:** Paul Attanasio
*Based on the book by Joseph D. Pistone and Richard Woodley*

## LAWRENCE OF ARABIA 1962, United Kingdom
**Director:** David Lean
**Cast:** Peter O'Toole, Alec Guinness, Anthony Quinn
**Screenplay:** T.E. Lawrence, Robert Bolt and Michael Wilson

## AN AMERICAN WEREWOLF IN LONDON 1981, USA
**Director:** John Landis
**Cast:** David Naughton, Jenny Agutter, Griffin Dunne
**Screenplay:** John Landis

## THE EVIL DEAD 1983, USA
**Director:** Sam Raimi
**Cast:** Bruce Campbell, Ellen Sandweiss
**Screenplay:** Sam Raimi

## THE EXORCIST 1973, USA
**Director:** William Friedkin **Cast:** Ellen Burstyn, Max von Sydow, Linda Blair
**Screenplay:** William Peter Blatty

## THE TEXAS CHAINSAW MASSACRE 1974, USA
**Director:** Tobe Hopper **Cast:** Marilyn Burns, Gunnar Hansen, Ed Neal
**Screenplay:** Kim Henkel and Tobe Hooper

Of course, you know, certain skeptics note that perhaps 10,000 of the nations's most elite highway patrolmen are out there waiting for us after we start, but let's stay positive: think of the fact that there's not one state in the 50 that has the death penalty for speeding . . . although I'm not so sure about Ohio.

– Look, your worshipfulness, let's get one thing straight.
I take orders from just one person: Me!
– It's a wonder you're still alive.

– For God's sake, Chris! The whole world is watching.
We can't let him die in front of a live audience!
– He was born in front of a live audience.

I think I need a root canal. I definitely need a long, slow root canal.

. . . Try to get this straight. There is nothing between us.
There has never been anything between us. Just air.

– What's your name? Come on. What's your name? Do you have a name? Do you have a police record? Where are you from?
– Disneyland.

## THE CANNONBALL RUN 1981, USA
**Director:** Hal Needham
**Cast:** Burt Reynolds, Roger Moore, Farrah Fawcett
**Screenplay:** Brock Yates

## STAR WARS 1977, USA
**Director:** George Lucas
**Cast:** Mark Hamill, Harrison Ford, Carrie Fisher
**Screenplay:** George Lucas

## THE TRUMAN SHOW 1998, USA
**Director:** Peter Weir
**Cast:** Jim Carrey, Laura Linney, Ed Harris
**Screenplay:** Andrew Niccol

## LITTLE SHOP OF HORRORS 1986, USA
**Director:** Frank Oz
**Cast:** Rick Moranis, Ellen Greene, Vincent Gardenia
**Screenplay:** Charles B. Griffith and Howard Ashman

## SINGIN' IN THE RAIN 1952, USA
**Director:** Gene Kelly, Stanley Donen
**Cast:** Gene Kelly, Debbie Reynolds, Donald O'Conner
**Screenplay:** Betty Comden and Adolph Green

## THE HITCHER 1986, USA
**Director:** Robert Harmon
**Cast:** Rutger Hauer, C. Thomas Howell, Jennifer Jason Leigh
**Screenplay:** Eric Red

– Now you don't sit down for two reasons,
either you scared or you just hate niggers.
– I'm not scared, I just hate niggers.

I have to remind myself that some birds aren't meant to be caged.
Their feathers are just too bright.

– Listen. Why don't we begin with what happened tonight, hmm?
Perhaps you could . . . you know, give me some of the details.
– I was here, Doc . . . died, you came.
– That's it?
– I'm a demon for details.

Keaton always said, "I don't believe in God, but I'm afraid of him." Well
I believe in God, and the only thing that scares me is Keyser Soze.

Why don't you knock it off with them negative waves? Why
don't you dig how beautiful it is out here? Why don't you say
something righteous and hopeful for a change?

Time marches on and sooner or later, you realize
it is marchin' across your face.

## ESCAPE FROM ALCATRAZ 1979, USA
**Director:** Donald Siegel
**Cast:** Clint Eastwood, Patrick McGoohan, Roberts Blossom
**Screenplay:** Richard Tuggle
*Based on the book by J. Campbell Bruce*

## THE SHAWSHANK REDEMPTION 1994, USA
**Director:** Frank Darabont
**Cast:** Tim Robbins, Morgan Freeman, Bob Gunton
**Screenplay:** Frank Darabont
*Based on the book by Stephen King*

## MARATHON MAN 1976, USA
**Director:** John Schlesinger
**Cast:** Dustin Hoffman, Laurence Olivier, Roy Scheider
**Screenplay:** William Goldman
*Based on the book by William Goldman*

## THE USUAL SUSPECTS 1995, USA
**Director:** Bryan Singer
**Cast:** Stephen Baldwin, Gabriel Byrne, Chazz Palminteri
**Screenplay:** Christopher McQuarrie

## KELLY'S HEROES 1970, USA
**Director:** Brian G. Hutton
**Cast:** Clint Eastwood, Telly Savalas, Don Rickles
**Screenplay:** Troy Kennedy-Martin

## STEEL MAGNOLIAS 1989, USA
**Director:** Herbert Ross
**Cast:** Sally Field, Dolly Parton, Julia Roberts
**Screenplay:** Robert Harling

– You gonna kill me, Snake?
– Not now, I'm too tired. Maybe later.


– Who's that then?
– I dunno. Must be a king.
– Why?
– He hasn't got shit all over him.


– You know where you're going?
– Uptown, I believe?
– Uptown? You headed into Harlem!
– Well you just stay on the tail of that jukebox and
there's an extra twenty dollars in it for you.
– Hey man, for twenty bucks, I'd take you to a Ku Klux Klan cookout!


Now comes the part where I relieve you, the little people, of the
burden of your failed and useless lives. But remember, as my plastic
surgeon always said: if you gotta go, go with a smile.


– You guys got nothing to worry about. I'm a professional.
– A professional what?

## ESCAPE FROM NEW YORK  1981, USA
**Director:** John Carpenter
**Cast:** Kurt Russell, Lee Van Cleef, Ernest Borgnine
**Screenplay:** John Carpenter and Nick Castle

## MONTY PYTHON AND THE HOLY GRAIL  1975, United Kingdom
**Director:** Terry Gilliam, Terry Jones
**Cast:** Graham Chapman, John Cleese, Terry Gilliam
**Screenplay:** Graham Chapman, John Cleese, Eric Idle, Terry Gilliam, Terry Jones
and Michael Palin

## LIVE AND LET DIE  1973, United Kingdom
**Director:** Guy Hamilton
**Cast:** Roger Moore, Yaphet Kotto, Jane Seymour
**Screenplay:** Tom Mankiewicz
*Based on the book by Ian Fleming*

## BATMAN  1989, USA
**Director:** Tim Burton
**Cast:** Jack Nicholson, Michael Keaton, Kim Basinger
**Screenplay:** Bob Kane, Sam Hamm and Warren Skaaren

## FERRIS BUELLER'S DAY OFF  1986, USA
**Director:** John Hughes
**Cast:** Matthew Broderick, Alan Ruck, Mia Sara
**Screenplay:** John Hughes

– You wanna go for a ride?
– No, thanks.
– No, thanks. What does that mean?
– I don't want to go.
– Go where?
– For a ride.
– A ride? Hell, that's a good idea.

A drug person can learn to cope with things like seeing their dead
grandmother crawling up their leg with a knife in her teeth.
But no one should be asked to handle this trip.

– Hollis seems to think you're an innocent man.
– Well, I've been accused of a lot of things before,
Mrs. Mulwray, but never that.

You were only supposed to blow the bloody doors off.

You are not machines, you are not cattle, you are men! You have the
love of humanity in your hearts! You don't hate! Only the unloved
hate; the unloved and the unnatural. Soldiers!

– Hey, hey, hey, baby! What do you say?
– Don't say anything and we'll get along just fine.

## BLUE VELVET 1986, USA
**Director:** David Lynch
**Cast:** Kyle MacLachlan, Isabella Rossellini, Dennis Hopper
**Screenplay:** David Lynch


## FEAR AND LOATHING IN LAS VEGAS 1998, USA
**Director:** Terry Gilliam
**Cast:** Johnny Depp, Benicio Del Toro, Tobey Maguire
**Screenplay:** Terry Gilliam, Tony Grisoni, Tod Davies and Alex Cox
*Based on the book by Hunter S. Thompson*

## CHINATOWN 1974, USA
**Director:** Roman Polanski
**Cast:** Jack Nicholson, Faye Dunaway, John Huston
**Screenplay:** Robert Towne and Roman Polanski

## THE ITALIAN JOB 1969, United Kingdom
**Director:** Peter Collinson
**Cast:** Michael Caine, Noel Coward, Maggie Blye
**Screenplay:** Troy Kennedy-Martin

## THE GREAT DICTATOR 1940, USA
**Director:** Charles Chaplin
**Cast:** Charles Chaplin, Jack Oakie, Reginald Gardiner
**Screenplay:** Charles Chaplin

## AMERICAN GRAFFITI 1973, USA
**Director:** George Lucas
**Cast:** Richard Dreyfuss, Ron Howard, Paul Le Mat
**Screenplay:** George Lucas, Gloria Katz and Willard Huyck

Even a poisonous snake isn't bad.
You just have to keep away from the sharp end.


Luke, you can destroy the Emperor. He has foreseen this.
It is your destiny. Join me, and together we
will rule the galaxy as father and son!


You don't understand. I coulda had class. I coulda been a
contender. I coulda been somebody, instead of a bum. Which
is what I am, let's face it. It was you, Charley.


I was married for four years, and pretended to be happy. And I
had six years of analysis, and pretended to be sane. My husband
ran off with his boyfriend, and I had an affair with my analyst,
who told me I was the worst lay he'd ever had.

I think voting is the opium of the masses in this country.
Every four years you deaden the pain.


Now hold it, hold it. We're about to accuse Haldeman,
who only happens to be the second most important man in
this country, of conducting a criminal conspiracy from inside
the White House. It would be nice if we were right.

## THE GODS MUST BE CRAZY 1981, Norway
**Director:** Jamie Uys
**Cast:** Marius Weyers, Sandra Prinsloo, N!xau
**Screenplay:** Jamie Uys

## THE EMPIRE STRIKES BACK 1980, USA
**Director:** Irwin Kershner
**Cast:** Mark Hamill, Harrison Ford, Carrie Fisher
**Screenplay:** George Lucas, Leigh Brackett and Lawrence Kasdan

## ON THE WATERFRONT 1954, USA
**Director:** Elia Kazan
**Cast:** Marlon Brando, Karl Malden, Rod Steiger
**Screenplay:** Bud Schulberg

## NETWORK 1976, USA
**Director:** Sidney Lumet
**Cast:** William Holden, Faye Dunaway, Peter Finch
**Screenplay:** Paddy Chayefsky

## REDS 1981, USA
**Director:** Warren Beatty
**Cast:** Warren Beatty, Diane Keaton, Edward Herrmann
**Screenplay:** Warren Beatty, Trevor Griffiths, Elaine May,
Jeremy Pikser and Peter S. Feibleman

## ALL THE PRESIDENT'S MEN 1976, USA
**Director:** Alan J. Pakula
**Cast:** Robert Redford, Dustin Hoffman, Jason Robards
**Screenplay:** William Goldman
*Based on the book by Carl Bernstein and Bob Woodward*

A good fight should be like a small play but played seriously. A good martial artist does not become tense, but ready. Not thinking, yet not dreaming. Ready for whatever may come. When the opponent expands, I contract. When he contracts, I expand. And when there is an opportunity, I do not hit! It hits all by itself.

– Who are these men?
– They're associated with Special Forces.
– What? What does that mean?
– It means that they are associated with Special Forces.

We're not students, we're The Ramones.

– Oh, the Indian is hot. I go for exotic types, especially when they're half-naked.
– Lulu!
– You tell him I'll make up for all the indignities they suffered in Roots.

– Don't take that tone with me, young man! I fought the war for your sort.
– I bet you're sorry you won.

Well, I've always believed that if done properly, armed robbery doesn't have to be an unpleasant experience.

## ENTER THE DRAGON 1973, USA
**Director:** Robert Clouse
**Cast:** Bruce Lee, John Saxon, Jim Kelly
**Screenplay:** Michael Allin


## NO WAY OUT 1987, USA
**Director:** Roger Donaldson
**Cast:** Kevin Costner, Gene Hackman, Sean Young
**Screenplay:** Robert Garland
*Based on the book by Kenneth Fearing*

## ROCK 'N' ROLL HIGH SCHOOL 1979, USA
**Director:** Allan Arkush, Joe Dante
**Cast:** P.J. Soles, Vincent Van Patten, Clint Howard
**Screenplay:** Richard Whitley and Russ Dvonch

## CAN'T STOP THE MUSIC 1980, USA
**Director:** Nancy Walker
**Cast:** Alex Briley, David Hodo, Glenn Hughes
**Screenplay:** Alan Carr and Bronte Woodard


## A HARD DAY'S NIGHT 1964, United Kingdom
**Director:** Richard Lester
**Cast:** John Lennon, Paul McCartney, George Harrison
**Screenplay:** Alun Owen

## THELMA & LOUISE 1991, USA
**Director:** Ridley Scott
**Cast:** Susan Sarandon, Geena Davis, Harvey Keitel
**Screenplay:** Callie Khouri

– I am awake.
– Your eyes are shut.
– Who you gonna believe?


– But what is so alarming about laughter?
– Laughter kills fear, and without fear there can be no faith,
because without fear of the Devil there is no more need of God.


When you love someone, you've gotta trust them. There's
no other way. You've got to give them the key to everything
that's yours. Otherwise, what's the point? And, for a while,
I believed that's the kind of love I had.


– He's a man from outer space and we're taking him
to his spaceship.
– Well, can't he just beam up?
– This is REALITY, Greg.

Like the sign says, speed's just a question of money.
How fast can you go?


I should've killed myself when he put it in me. After the first time,
before we were married, Ralph promised never again. He promised,
and I believed him. But sin never dies. Sin never dies.

## MILLER'S CROSSING 1990, USA
**Director:** Joel Coen
**Cast:** Gabriel Byrne, Albert Finney, Marcia Gay Harden
**Screenplay:** Joel Coen and Ethan Coen
*Based on the book by Dashiell Hammett*

## THE NAME OF THE ROSE 1986, France/Italy/West Germany
**Director:** Jean Jacques Annaud
**Cast:** Sean Connery, F. Murray Abraham, Christian Slater
**Screenplay:** Andrew Birkin, Gérard Brach, Howard Franklin and Alain Godard
*Based on the book by Umberto Eco*

## CASINO 1995, USA
**Director:** Martin Scorsese
**Cast:** Robert De Niro, Sharon Stone, Joe Pesci
**Screenplay:** Nicholas Pileggi and Martin Scorsese
*Based on the book by Nicholas Pileggi*

## E.T. THE EXTRA-TERRESTRIAL 1982, USA
**Director:** Steven Spielberg
**Cast:** Dee Wallace, Henry Thomas, Peter Coyote
**Screenplay:** Melissa Mathison

## MAD MAX 1979, Australia
**Director:** George Miller
**Cast:** Mel Gibson, Joanne Samuel, Hugh Keays Byrne
**Screenplay:** James McCausland and George Miller

## CARRIE 1976, USA
**Director:** Brian De Palma
**Cast:** Sissy Spacek, Piper Laurie, William Katt
**Screenplay:** Lawrence D. Cohen
*Based on the book by Stephen King*

– Is there something bad here?
– Well, you know, Doc, when something happens, you can leave a trace of itself behind. Say like, if someone burns toast. Well, maybe things that happen leave other kinds of traces behind. Not things that anyone can notice, but things that people who shine can see . . .

Normally, both your asses would be dead as fucking fried chicken, but you happen to pull this shit while I'm in a transitional period so I don't wanna kill you, I wanna help you. But I can't give you this case, it don't belong to me. Besides, I've already been through too much shit this morning over this case to hand it over to your dumb ass.

Queen Elizabeth is a man! Prince Charles is a faggot!
Winston Churchill was full of shit! Shakespeare's French!

– Why are you laughing?
– You're going to rent cars?!
– That's right, I know a lot about cars.
I've been stealing them since I was fourteen.

– Monsieur Rick, what kind of a man is Captain Renault?
– Oh, he's just like any other man, only more so.

## THE SHINING  1980, USA
**Director:** Stanley Kubrick
**Cast:** Jack Nicholson, Shelley Duvall, Danny Lloyd
**Screenplay:** Stanley Kubrick and Diane Johnson
*Based on the book by Stephen King*

## HALLOWEEN  1978, USA
**Director:** John Carpenter
**Cast:** Donald Pleasence, Jamie Lee Curtis
**Screenplay:** John Carpenter and Debra Hill

## AN AMERICAN WEREWOLF IN LONDON  1981, USA
**Director:** John Landis
**Cast:** David Naughton, Jenny Agutter, Griffin Dunne
**Screenplay:** John Landis

## CARLITO'S WAY  1993, USA
**Director:** Brian De Palma
**Cast:** Al Pacino, Sean Penn, Penelope Ann Miller
**Screenplay:** David Koepp
*Based on the book by Edwin Torres*

## CASABLANCA  1942, USA
**Director:** Michael Curtiz
**Cast:** Humphrey Bogart, Ingrid Bergman, Paul Henreid
**Screenplay:** Murray Burnett, Joan Alison, Julius J. Epstein, Philip G. Epstein,
    Howard Koch and Casey Robinson

Speed is like a dozen transatlantic flights without ever getting off the plane. Time change. You lose, you gain. Makes no difference so long as you keep taking the pills. But sooner or later, you've got to get out because it's crashing, and then all at once the frozen hours melt out through the nervous system and seep out the pores.

Normally, both your asses would be dead as fucking fried chicken, but you happen to pull this shit while I'm in a transitional period so I don't wanna kill you, I wanna help you. But I can't give you this case, it don't belong to me. Besides, I've already been through too much shit this morning over this case to hand it over to your dumb ass.

Most people don't know how they're gonna feel from one moment to the next. But a dope fiend has a pretty good idea. All you gotta do is look at the labels on the little bottles.

– He's pissed at YOU, Wirf.
– Only because he knows I won't go away.
– I know how he feels.

This is your life and it's ending one minute at a time.

– Are you looking to lose weight, or do you want increased strength and flexibility as well?
– I want to look good naked!

## WITHNAIL AND I  1987, United Kingdom
**Director:** Bruce Robinson
**Cast:** Richard E. Grant, Paul McGann, Richard Griffiths
**Screenplay:** Bruce Robinson


## PULP FICTION  1994, USA
**Director:** Quentin Tarantino
**Cast:** John Travolta, Samuel L. Jackson, Uma Thurman
**Screenplay:** Quentin Tarantino and Roger Avary


## DRUGSTORE COWBOY  1989, USA
**Director:** Gus Van Sant
**Cast:** Matt Dillon, Kelly Lynch, James Remar
**Screenplay:** Gus Van Sant, Daniel Yost and William S. Burroughs
*Based on the book by James Fogle*

## NOBODY'S FOOL  1994, USA
**Director:** Robert Benton
**Cast:** Paul Newman, Jessica Tandy, Bruce Willis
**Screenplay:** Robert Benton
*Based on the book by Richard Russo*

## FIGHT CLUB  1999, USA
**Director:** David Fincher
**Cast:** Brad Pitt, Edward Norton, Helena Bonham Carter
**Screenplay:** Jim Uhls
*Based on the book by Chuck Palahniuk*

## AMERICAN BEAUTY  1999, USA
**Director:** Sam Mendes  **Cast:** Kevin Spacey, Annette Bening, Thora Birch
**Screenplay:** Alan Ball

– Captain Hawkeye Pierce. I got a TWX about you.
It seems you stole a Jeep up at headquarters.
– Oh no no, no, sir, I did not steal a Jeep.
No, it's, uh, right outside. Right there.

– . . . I would suggest that those of us with stout hearts
and trim waistlines, start using the stairs.
– That's 135 floors.
– All downhill.

– I saw a young officer on deck the other day, and he looked
DAMN familiar . . . even with his clothes on!
– So . . . he recognized ya, so?
– So doesn't that bother you?
– If it bothered me, I wouldn't have married ya.
– Well, first you arrested me six times!
– Well, I had to figure out some way to keep
you off the streets until you'd marry me!

I'm loud, darling, but never cheap.

At birth, I was cast into a flaming pit of scum forgotten by God.

Neighbors bring food with death, and flowers with sickness,
and little things in between . . .

## MASH 1970, USA
**Director:** Robert Altman
**Cast:** Donald Sutherland, Elliott Gould, Tom Skerritt
**Screenplay:** Ring Lardner Jr. *Based on the book by Richard Hooker*

## THE TOWERING INFERNO 1974, USA
**Director:** John Guillermin, Irwin Allen
**Cast:** Steve McQueen, Paul Newman, William Holden
**Screenplay:** Stirling Silliphant
*Based on the book by Richard Martin Stern, Thomas N. Scortia
and Frank M. Robinson*

## THE POSEIDON ADVENTURE 1972, USA
**Director:** Ronald Neame
**Cast:** Gene Hackman, Ernest Borgnine, Red Buttons
**Screenplay:** Wendell Mayes and Stirling Silliphant
*Based on the book by Paul Gallico*

## THE CRYING GAME 1992, United Kingdom
**Director:** Neil Jordan **Cast:** Stephan Rea, Miranda Richardson, Forest Whitaker
**Screenplay:** Neil Jordan

## NATURAL BORN KILLERS 1994, USA
**Director:** Oliver Stone **Cast:** Woody Harrelson, Juliette Lewis, Robert Downey Jr.
**Screenplay:** Quentin Tarantino, David Veloz, Richard Rutowski and Oliver Stone

## TO KILL A MOCKINGBIRD 1962, USA
**Director:** Robert Mulligan
**Cast:** Gregory Peck, Mary Badham, Philip Alford
**Screenplay:** Horton Foote *Based on the book by Harper Lee*

– You know, we are sitting here, you and I, like a couple of regular fellas. You do what you do, and I do what I gotta do. And now that we've been face to face, if I'm there and I gotta put you away, I won't like it. But I tell you, if it's between you and some poor bastard whose wife you're gonna turn into a widow, brother, you are going down.
– There is a flip side to that coin. What if you do got me boxed in and I gotta put you down? Cause no matter what, you will not get in my way. We've been face to face, yeah. But I will not hesitate. Not for a second.

– We split that.
– How the fuck do you split a car, you dummy?
With a fucking chainsaw?

– I'm a marked man in this department. For what?
– I've already arranged a transfer for you.
– To where? China?

Go ahead, punk, make my day.

– Water polo? Isn't that terribly dangerous?
– I'll say. I had two ponies drowned under me.

– The mirror . . . it's broken!
– Yes, I know. I like it that way. Makes me look the way I feel.

## HEAT  1995, USA
**Director:** Michael Mann
**Cast:** Al Pacino, Robert De Niro, Val Kilmer
**Screenplay:** Michael Mann

## FARGO  1996, USA
**Director:** Joel Coen  **Cast:** Frances McDormand, William H. Macy, Steve Buscemi
**Screenplay:** Joel Coen and Ethan Coen

## SERPICO  1973, USA
**Director:** Sidney Lumet
**Cast:** Al Pacino, John Randolph, Jack Kehoe
**Screenplay:** Waldo Salt and Norman Wexler  *Based on the book by Peter Maas*

## DIRTY HARRY  1971, USA
**Director:** Don Siegal
**Cast:** Clint Eastwood, Harry Guardino, Reni Santoni
**Screenplay:** Harry Julian Fink, Rita M. Fink, Dean Riesner and John Milius

## SOME LIKE IT HOT  1959, USA
**Director:** Billy Wilder
**Cast:** Jack Lemmon, Tony Curtis, Marilyn Monroe
**Screenplay:** Robert Thoeren, M. Logan, Billy Wilder and I.A.L. Diamond

## THE APARTMENT  1960, USA
**Director:** Billy Wilder
**Cast:** Jack Lemmon, Shirley MacLaine, Fred MacMurray
**Screenplay:** Billy Wilder and I.A.L. Diamond

– Ahem, look. Sorry, sorry. I just, ahem. Well, this is a very stupid question and . . . particularly in view of our recent shopping excursion, but I just wondered, by any chance, ahem, eh, I mean obviously not because I guess I've only slept with nine people, but but I-I just wondered . . . ehh. I really feel, ehh, in short, to recap it slightly in a clearer version, eh, the words of David Cassidy in fact, eh, while he was still with the Partridge family, eh, I think I love you, and eh, I-I just wondered by any chance you wouldn't like to . . . eh . . . eh . . . no, no, no of course not . . . I'm an idiot, he's not . . . Excellent, excellent. Fantastic. Eh, I was gonna say lovely to see you, sorry to disturb . . . better get on . . .
– That was very romantic.
– Well, I thought it over a lot, you know, I wanted to get it just right.

I love you more than any woman's ever loved a rabbit.

They drew first blood, not me. They drew first blood.

– She's wonderful! Wherever did you find her?
– 976-BABE.

Now I have a machine gun. Ho ho ho.

I don't mind a reasonable amount of trouble.

## FOUR WEDDINGS AND A FUNERAL  1994, United Kingdom
**Director:** Mike Newell
**Cast:** Hugh Grant, Andie MacDowell, Kristin Scott Thomas
**Screenplay:** Richard Curtis

## WHO FRAMED ROGER RABBIT   1988, USA
**Director:** Robert Zemeckis  **Cast:** Bob Hoskins, Christopher Lloyd, Joanna Cassidy
**Screenplay:** Jeffrey Price and Peter S. Seaman  *Based on the book by Gary K. Wolf*

## FIRST BLOOD  1982, USA
**Director:** Ted Kotcheff  **Cast:** Sylvester Stallone, Richard Crenna, Brian Dennehy
**Screenplay:** Michael Kozoll, William Sackheim, Sylvester Stallone
*Based on the book by David Morrell*

## PRETTY WOMAN  1990, USA
**Director:** Garry Marshall  **Cast:** Richard Gere, Julia Roberts, Ralph Bellamy
**Screenplay:** J.F. Lawton

## DIE HARD  1988, USA
**Director:** John McTiernan  **Cast:** Bruce Willis, Alan Rickman, Bonnie Bedelia
**Screenplay:** Jeb Stuart and Steven E. de Souza  *Based on the book by Roderick Thorp*

## THE MALTESE FALCON  1941, USA
**Director:** John Huston  **Cast:** Humphrey Bogart, Mary Astor, Peter Lorre
**Screenplay:** John Huston  *Based on the book by Dashiell Hammett*

Hey look, mister. We serve hard drinks in here for men who want to get drunk fast and we don't need any characters around to give the joint atmosphere. Is that clear, or do I have to slip you my left for a convincer?

– Where were you last night?
– That's so long ago, I don't remember.
– Will I see you tonight?
– I never make plans that far ahead.

– Can you imagine the kind of life he must have had?
– Yes, I think I can.
– No, I don't think so. No one could possibly imagine it!
I don't believe any of us can!

– Doesn't it hurt?
– Well, I sort of lay there in pain, but I love it. I really love it. I lay there hovering between consciousness and unconsciousness.
It's really the greatest.

– Oh no, you can't take my photograph.
– Oh, I'm sorry, you believe it will take your spirit away?
– No, you got lens-cap on it.

## IT'S A WONDERFUL LIFE 1946, USA
**Director:** Frank Capra
**Cast:** James Stewart, Donna Reed, Lionel Barrymore
**Screenplay:** Philip Van Doren Stern, Frances Goodrich, Albert
  Hackett, Frank Capra, Jo Swerling and Michael Wilson

## CASABLANCA 1942, USA
**Director:** Michael Curtiz
**Cast:** Humphrey Bogart, Ingrid Bergman, Paul Henreid
**Screenplay:** Murray Burnett, Joan Alison, Julius J. Epstein, Philip G. Epstein,
  Howard Koch and Casey Robinson

## THE ELEPHANT MAN 1980, USA
**Director:** David Lynch
**Cast:** Anthony Hopkins, John Hurt, Anne Bancroft
**Screenplay:** Christopher De Vore, Eric Bergren and David Lynch
*Based on the book by Sir Frederick Treves and Ashley Montagu*

## LOLITA 1962, United Kingdom
**Director:** Stanley Kubrick
**Cast:** James Mason, Shelley Winters, Peter Sellers
**Screenplay:** Vladimir Nabokov and Stanley Kubrick
*Based on the book by Vladimir Nabokov*

## CROCODILE DUNDEE 1986, Australia
**Director:** Peter Faiman
**Cast:** Paul Hogan, Linda Kozlowski, John Meillon
**Screenplay:** John Cornell, Paul Hogan and Ken Shadie

We had two bags of grass, seventy-five pellets of mescaline, five sheets of high powered blotter acid, a salt shaker half full of cocaine and a whole galaxy of multicolored uppers, downers, laughers, screamers . . . Also a quart of tequilla, a quart of rum, a case of beer, a pint of raw ether, and two dozen amyls. Not that we needed all that for the trip, but once you get locked into a serious drug collection, the tendency is to push it as far as you can. The only thing that really worried me was the ether. There is nothing in the world more helpless and irresponsible and depraved than a man in the depths of an ether binge. And I knew we'd get into that rotten stuff pretty soon.

You know something, Verna? If I turn my back for long enough for Big Ed to put a hole in it, there'd be a hole in it.

God is not on our side because he hates idiots, also.

Life goes by pretty fast. If you don't stop and look around once in a while, you could miss it.

You know, you guys are amazing. You think not getting caught in a lie is the same thing as telling the truth!

– Nice beaver!
– Thank you. I just had it stuffed.

## FEAR AND LOATHING IN LAS VEGAS  1998, USA
**Director:** Terry Gilliam
**Cast:** Johnny Depp, Benicio Del Toro, Tobey Maguire
**Screenplay:** Terry Gilliam, Tony Grisoni, Tod Davies and Alex Cox
*Based on the book by Hunter S. Thompson*

## WHITE HEAT  1949, USA
**Director:** Raoul Walsh  **Cast:** James Cagney, Virginia Mayo, Edmond O'Brien
**Screenplay:** Virginia Kellogg, Ivan Goff and Ben Roberts

## THE GOOD, THE BAD, AND THE UGLY  1966, Italy
**Director:** Sergio Leone  **Cast:** Clint Eastwood, Lee Van Cleef, Eli Wallach
**Screenplay:** Luciano Vincenzoni, Sergio Leone, Agenore Incrocci and Furio Scarpelli

## FERRIS BUELLER'S DAY OFF  1986, USA
**Director:** John Hughes  **Cast:** Matthew Broderick, Alan Ruck, Mia Sara
**Screenplay:** John Hughes

## THREE DAYS OF THE CONDOR  1975, USA
**Director:** Sydney Pollack
**Cast:** Robert Redford, Faye Dunaway, Cliff Robertson
**Screenplay:** Lorenzo Semple Jr. and David Rayfiel  *Based on the book by James Grady*

## THE NAKED GUN: FROM THE FILES OF POLICE SQUAD  1988, USA
**Director:** David Zucker
**Cast:** Leslie Nielsen, George Kennedy, Priscilla Presley
**Screenplay:** Jim Abrahams, David Zucker and Pat Proft

I think now, looking back, we did not fight the enemy. We fought ourselves. The enemy was in us. The war is over for me now, but it will always be there, the rest of my days. As I'm sure Elias will be, fighting with Barnes for what Rhah called possession of my soul. There are times since, I've felt like a child, born of those two fathers. But be that as it may, those of us who did make it have an obligation to build again. To teach to others what we know, and to try with what's left of our lives to find a goodness and a meaning to this life.

– Alright. I'll do it. I'will show you how a Prussian officer fights.
– And I will show you where the Iron Crosses grow.

. . . The greatest trick the devil ever pulled was convincing the world he didn't exist . . .

You make me sick with your heroics. There's a stench of death about you. You carry it in your pack like the plague.

My mother told me to never do this.

She just goes a little mad sometimes. We all go a little mad sometimes. Haven't you?

## PLATOON 1986, USA
**Director:** Oliver Stone
**Cast:** Tom Berenger, Willem Dafoe, Charlie Sheen
**Screenplay:** Oliver Stone

## CROSS OF IRON 1977, United Kingdom/West Germany
**Director:** Sam Peckinpah
**Cast:** James Coburn, Maximilian Schell, James Mason
**Screenplay:** Julius J. Epstein, James Hamilton and Walter Kelley
*Based on the book by Willi Heinrich*

## THE USUAL SUSPECTS 1995, USA
**Director:** Bryan Singer
**Cast:** Stephen Baldwin, Gabriel Byrne, Chazz Palminteri
**Screenplay:** Christopher McQuarrie

## THE BRIDGE ON THE RIVER KWAI 1957, United Kingdom
**Director:** David Lean
**Cast:** William Holden, Alec Guinness, Jack Hawkins
**Screenplay:** Michael Wilson and Carl Foreman *Based on the book by Pierre Boulle*

## THE HITCHER 1986, USA
**Director:** Robert Harmon
**Cast:** Rutger Hauer, C. Thomas Howell, Jennifer Jason Leigh
**Screenplay:** Eric Red

## PSYCHO 1960, USA
**Director:** Alfred Hitchcock  **Cast:** Anthony Perkins, Janet Leigh, Vera Miles
**Screenplay:** Joseph Stefano *Based on the book by Robert Bloch*

– I only have sex with a guy for money.
– Yeah, I know.
– And two guys can't love each other.
– Yeah. Well, I don't know. I mean . . . I mean for me, I could love someone even if I, you know, wasn't paid for it. I love you and . . . you don't pay me.

And maybe there's no peace in this world. For us or for anyone else, I don't know. But I do know that, as long as we live, we must remain true to ourselves.

You wanna know how to get Capone? They pull a knife, you pull a gun. He sends one of yours to the hospital, you send on of his to the morgue. *That's* the *Chicago* way. And that's how you get Capone. Now, do you want to do that? Are you ready to do that?

– You'll live with the stink of the streets all your life.
– I like the stink of the streets. It cleans out my lungs. And it gives me a hard-on.

You don't make up for your sins in church. You do it in the streets. You do it at home. The rest is bullshit and you know it.

Favor gonna kill you faster than a bullet.

## MY OWN PRIVATE IDAHO 1991, USA
**Director:** Gus Van Sant
**Cast:** River Phoenix, Keanu Reeves, James Russo
**Screenplay:** Gus Van Sant

## SPARTACUS 1960, USA
**Director:** Stanley Kubrick **Cast:** Kirk Douglas, Laurence Olivier, Jean Simmons
**Screenplay:** Dalton Trumbo, Calder Willingham and Peter Ustinov
*Based on the book by Howard Fast*

## THE UNTOUCHABLES 1987, USA
**Director:** Brian De Palma
**Cast:** Kevin Costner, Sean Connery, Charles Martin Smith
**Screenplay:** David Mamet
*Based on the book by Oscar Fraley and Eliot Ness*

## ONCE UPON A TIME IN AMERICA 1984, USA
**Director:** Sergio Leone **Cast:** Robert De Niro, James Woods, Elizabeth McGovern
**Screenplay:** Leonardo Benvenuti, Piero De Bernardi, Enrico Medioli, Franco Arcalli,
    Franco Ferrini, Sergio Leone, Stuart Kaminsky and Ernesto Gastaldi
*Based on the book by Harry Grey*

## MEAN STREETS 1973, USA
**Director:** Martin Scorsese
**Cast:** Robert De Niro, Harvey Keitel, David Proval
**Screenplay:** Martin Scorsese and Mardik Martin

## CARLITO'S WAY 1993, USA
**Director:** Brian De Palma
**Cast:** Al Pacino, Sean Penn, Penelope Ann Miller
**Screenplay:** David Koepp *Based on the book by Edwin Torres*

– What if I were to call the police and tell them there's a bloke stay-
ing in me hotel that's planning to shoot somebody?
– You wouldn't do that.
– Why not?
– Because I know you wear purple underwear.
– And what's that supposed to mean?
– Think about it.

I know it was you, Fredo. You broke my heart.
You broke my heart.

– . . . What's your last name?
– Same as my mother's and father's.
– And what's that?
– Which one? My mother's or my father's?
– Either!
– The same as mine!

I always like a little pussy after lunch.

Did you lose your mind all at once,
or was it a slow, gradual process?

## GET CARTER 1971, United Kingdom
**Director:** Mike Hodges
**Cast:** Michael Caine, Ian Hendry, Britt Ekland
**Screenplay:** Mike Hodges
*Based on the book by Ted Lewis*

## THE GODFATHER PART II 1974, USA
**Director:** Francis Ford Coppola
**Cast:** Al Pacino, Robert De Niro, Robert Duvall,
**Screenplay:** Mario Puzo and Francis Ford Coppola

## XANADU 1980, USA
**Director:** Robert Greenwald
**Cast:** Olivia Newton-John, Gene Kelly, Michael Beck
**Screenplay:** Richard Christian Danus and Marc Reid Rubel

## THE WITCHES OF EASTWICK 1987, USA
**Director:** George Miller
**Cast:** Jack Nicholson, Cher, Susan Sarandon
**Screenplay:** Michael Cristofer
*Based on the book by John Updike*

## THE FISHER KING 1991, USA
**Director:** Terry Gilliam
**Cast:** Robin Williams, Jeff Bridges, Amanda Plummer
**Screenplay:** Richard LaGravenese

Picture the best orgasm you ever had. Multiply it by
a thousand and you're still nowhere near it.




You're a strange person, Robert. I mean, what will you come to?
If a person has no love for himself, no respect for himself, no love of
his friends, family, work, something—how can he ask for love
in return? I mean, why should he ask for it?

– I wonder how such a degenerated person ever reached a
position of authority in the Army Medical Corps!
– He was drafted.




Miriam! I have to take your blood pressure!
I've been sitting still for 25 years. You missed your chance.




– Can't help it! A girl has her feelings.
– But, Dil, you're not a girl.
– Details, baby, Details.

## TRAINSPOTTING 1996, United Kingdom
**Director:** Danny Boyle
**Cast:** Ewan McGregor, Ewan Bremmer, Jonny Lee Miller
**Screenplay:** John Hodge
*Based on the book by Irvine Welsh*

## FIVE EASY PIECES 1970, USA
**Director:** Bob Rafelson
**Cast:** Jack Nicholson, Karen Black, Billy Green Bush
**Screenplay:** Carole Eastman and Bob Rafelson

## MASH 1970, USA
**Director:** Robert Altman
**Cast:** Donald Sutherland, Elliott Gould, Tom Skerritt
**Screenplay:** Ring Lardner Jr.
*Based on the book by Richard Hooker*

## AWAKENINGS 1990, USA
**Director:** Penny Marshall
**Cast:** Robert De Niro, Robin Williams, Julie Kavner
**Screenplay:** Steven Zaillian
*Based on the book by Oliver Sacks*

## THE CRYING GAME 1992, United Kingdom
**Director:** Neil Jordan
**Cast:** Stephan Rea, Miranda Richardson, Forest Whitaker
**Screenplay:** Neil Jordan

Once upon a time, a woman was picking up firewood. She came upon a poisonous snake frozen in the snow. She took the snake home and nursed it back to health. One day the snake bit her on the cheek. As she lay dying, she asked the snake, Why have you done this to me? And the snake answersed, Look, bitch, you knew I was a snake.

Frank, let's face it. Who can trust a cop that won't take money?

– I come from a musical family. My mother is a piano teacher and my father was a conductor.
– Where did he conduct?
– On the Baltimore and Ohio.

Ya know, I used to live like Robinson and Crusoe. I mean, shipwrecked among 8 million people. And then one day I saw a footprint in the sand and there you were.

There comes a time that a piano realizes that it has not written a concerto.

The point is, ladies and gentlemen, that greed, for lack of a better word, is good. Greed is right. Greed works.

## NATURAL BORN KILLERS  1994, USA
**Director:** Oliver Stone
**Cast:** Woody Harrelson, Juliette Lewis, Robert Downey Jr.
**Screenplay:** Quentin Tarantino, David Veloz, Richard Rutowski and Oliver Stone

## SERPICO  1973, USA
**Director:** Sidney Lumet
**Cast:** Al Pacino, John Randolph, Jack Kehoe
**Screenplay:** Waldo Salt and Norman Wexler
*Based on the book by Peter Maas*

## SOME LIKE IT HOT  1959, USA
**Director:** Billy Wilder
**Cast:** Jack Lemmon, Tony Curtis, Marilyn Monroe
**Screenplay:** Robert Thoeren, M. Logan, Billy Wilder and I.A.L. Diamond

## THE APARTMENT  1960, USA
**Director:** Billy Wilder
**Cast:** Jack Lemmon, Shirley MacLaine, Fred MacMurray
**Screenplay:** Billy Wilder and I.A.L. Diamond

## ALL ABOUT EVE  1950, USA
**Director:** Joseph L. Mankiewicz
**Cast:** Bette Davis, Anne Baxter, George Sanders
**Screenplay:** Joseph L. Mankiewicz and Mary Orr

## WALL STREET  1987, USA
**Director:** Oliver Stone
**Cast:** Michael Douglas, Charlie Sheen, Daryl Hannah
**Screenplay:** Stanley Weiser and Oliver Stone

Class isn't something you buy. Look at you. You've got on a 500-dollar suit and you're still a low-life.

– Then you jump first.
– No, I said.
– What's the matter with you?
– I can't swim.
– Why, you crazy? The fall will probably kill you.

Try to imagine all life as you know it stopping instantaneously and every molecule in your body exploding at the speed of light.

What we were after now was the old surprise visit. That was a real kick and good for laughs and lashings of the old ultraviolence.

He's got a client who shot his wife in the head six times. Six times. Can you imagine it? I mean, even twice would be overdoing it, don't you think?

– We're more likely to believe an important local businessman than some foul-mouth jerk from out of town.
– Foul-mouth? Fuck you, man.

## 48 HRS. 1982, USA
**Director:** Walter Hill
**Cast:** Nick Nolte, Eddie Murphy, Annette O'Toole
**Screenplay:** Roger Spottiswoode, Walter Hill, Larry Gross
Steven E. de Souza and Jeb Stuart

## BUTCH CASSIDY AND THE SUNDANCE KID 1969, USA
**Director:** George Roy Hill
**Cast:** Paul Newman, Robert Redford, Katharine Ross
**Screenplay:** William Goldman

## GHOSTBUSTERS 1984, USA
**Director:** Ivan Reitman
**Cast:** Bill Murray, Dan Aykroyd, Harold Ramis
**Screenplay:** Dan Aykroyd, Harold Ramis and Rick Moranis

## A CLOCKWORK ORANGE 1971, USA
**Director:** Stanley Kubrick
**Cast:** Malcolm McDowell, Patrick Magee, Adrienne Corri
**Screenplay:** Stanley Kubrick
*Based on the book by Anthony Burgess*

## THE BIRDS 1963, USA
**Director:** Alfred Hitchcock
**Cast:** Rod Taylor, Tippi Hedren, Jessica Tandy
**Screenplay:** Daphne Du Maurier and Evan Hunter

## BEVERLY HILLS COP 1984, USA
**Director:** Martin Brest
**Cast:** Eddie Murphy, Judge Reinhold, John Ashton
**Screenplay:** Danilo Bach and Daniel Petrie Jr.

Back there, I could fly a gunship. I could drive a tank. I was in charge of million dollar equipment. Back here, I can't even hold a job parking cars!

– How odd that it should end this way for us, after so many stimulating encounters. I almost regret it. Where shall I find a new adversary so close to my own level?
– Try the local sewer.

– If you were not a bride, I would kiss you goodbye.
– If I were not a bride, there would be no goodbyes to be said.

– Sorta wish you hadn't done that, Hildy.
– Done what?
– Divorced me. Makes a fella lose all faith in himself. Gives him a . . . almost gives him a feeling he wasn't wanted.

– Man who catch fly with chopstick accomplish anything.
– Ever catch one?
– Not yet.

## FIRST BLOOD 1982, USA
**Director:** Ted Kotcheff
**Cast:** Sylvester Stallone, Richard Crenna, Brian Dennehy
**Screenplay:** Michael Kozoll, William Sackheim, Sylvester Stallone
*Based on the book by David Morrell*

## RAIDERS OF THE LOST ARK 1981, USA
**Director:** Steven Spielberg
**Cast:** Harrison Ford, Karen Allen, Wolf Kahler
**Screenplay:** George Lucas, Philip Kaufman and Lawrence Kasdan

## BEN-HUR 1959, USA
**Director:** William Wyler
**Cast:** Charlton Heston, Jack Hawkins, Stephen Boyd
**Screenplay:** Karl Tunberg, Maxwell Anderson, Christopher Fry and Gore Vidal
*Based on the book by Lew Wallace*

## HIS GIRL FRIDAY 1940, USA
**Director:** Howard Hawks
**Cast:** Cary Grant, Rosalind Russell, Ralph Bellamy
**Screenplay:** Ben Hecht, Charles MacArthur and Charles Lederer

## THE KARATE KID 1984, USA
**Director:** John G. Avildsen
**Cast:** Ralph Macchio, Noriyuki Morita, Elisabeth Shue
**Screenplay:** Robert Mark Kamen

– Excuse me. What is your name?
I'm Bob Woodward, of the *Washington Post*.
– Markham.
– Markham. Mr. Markham, are you here
in connection withthe Watergate burglary?
– I'm not here.

If I die, I'm sorry for all the bad things I did to you. And if I
live, I'm sorry for all the bad things I'm gonna do to you.

Well, obviously, those three girls
were just the wrong three girls.

– What do you play?
– I used to play football in school.
– I mean, what instrument?
– I don't.
– Then what are you doing here?
– Well, I saw everyone else lining up so, uh—I thought
you were selling drugs.

And crawling on this planet's face, some insects . . . called the
human race. Lost in time. And lost in space . . . and meaning.

– Cosmo, call me a cab.
– OK, you're a cab.

## ALL THE PRESIDENT'S MEN 1976, USA
**Director:** Alan J. Pakula
**Cast:** Robert Redford, Dustin Hoffman, Jason Roberts
**Screenplay:** William Goldman
*Based on the book by Carl Bernstein and Bob Woodward*


## ALL THAT JAZZ 1979, USA
**Director:** Bob Fosse
**Cast:** Roy Scheider, Jessica Lange, Ann Reinking
**Screenplay:** Robert Alan Aurthur and Bob Fosse

## CABARET 1972, USA
**Director:** Bob Fosse  **Cast:** Liza Minnelli, Michael York, Helmut Griem
**Screenplay:** John Van Druten, Joe Masteroff and Jay Presson Allen
*Based on the book by Christopher Isherwood*

## THE COMMITMENTS 1991, Ireland/UK/USA
**Director:** Alan Parker
**Cast:** Robert Arkins, Michael Aherne, Angeline Ball
**Screenplay:** Dick Clement, Ian La Frenais and Roddy Doyle
*Based on the book by Roddy Doyle*


## THE ROCKY HORROR PICTURE SHOW 1975, USA
**Director:** Jim Sharman  **Cast:** Tim Curry, Susan Sarandon, Barry Bostwick
**Screenplay:** Richard O'Brien, Jim Sharman

## SINGIN' IN THE RAIN 1952, USA
**Director:** Gene Kelly, Stanley Donen
**Cast:** Gene Kelly, Debbie Reynolds, Donald O'Connor
**Screenplay:** Betty Comden and Adolph Green

Survival kit contents check. In them, you'll find: one .45 caliber auto-
matic; two boxes of ammunition; four days concentrated emergency
rations; one drug issue containing: antibiotics, morphine, vitamin
pills, pep pills, sleeping pills, tranquilizer pills; one miniature combination Russian phrase book and bible; one hundred dollars in rubles;
one hundred dollars in gold; nine packs of chewing gum; one issue of
prophylactics; three lipsticks; three pair of nylon stockings. Shoot, a
fellah could have a pretty good weekend in Vegas with all that stuff.

It looks, after all, as if you will see Berlin before I do.

Don't feel bad about losing your virtue. I sort of knew
you would. Everybody always does.

– Have you any famous last words?
– Not yet.
– Not yet? Is that famous?

– Do you believe in God, Sargeant?
– I believe God is a sadist, but probably doesn't even know it.

– You forgive me?
– Nothing to forgive, Sydney. Nothing.

## DR. STRANGELOVE OR: HOW I LEARNED TO STOP WORRYING AND LOVE THE BOMB 1964, USA

**Director:** Stanley Kubrick
**Cast:** Peter Sellers, George C. Scott, Sterling Hayden
**Screenplay:** Stanley Kubrick, Terry Southern and Peter George III
*Based on the book by Peter George*

## THE GREAT ESCAPE 1963, USA

**Director:** John Sturges, **Cast:** Steve McQueen, James Garner, Richard Attenborough
**Screenplay:** James Clavell and W.R. Burnett
*Based on the book by Paul Brickhill*

## KLUTE 1971, USA

**Director:** Alan J. Pakula **Cast:** Jane Fonda, Donald Sutherland, Charles Cioffi
**Screenplay:** Andy Lewis and Dave Lewis

## THE ADVENTURES OF BARON MUNCHAUSEN 1989, United Kingdom

**Director:** Terry Gilliam **Cast:** John Neville, Eric Idle, Sarah Polley
**Screenplay:** Terry Gilliam and Charles McKeown
*Based on the book by Rudolph Erich Raspe*

## CROSS OF IRON 1977, United Kingdom/West Germany

**Director:** Sam Peckinpah
**Cast:** James Coburn, Maximilian Schell, James Mason
**Screenplay:** Julius J. Epstein, James Hamilton and Walter Kelley
*Based on the book by Willi Heinrich*

## THE KILLING FIELDS 1984, United Kingdom

**Director:** Roland Joffe **Cast:** Sam Waterston, Haing S. Ngor, John Malkovich
**Screenplay:** Bruce Robinson

– Somewhere out there is the beast and he's hungry tonight.
– Have you ever gotten into a mistake that
you just can't get out of, King?
– There is a way out of everything, man. Just keep your
pecker hard and your powder dry and the world will turn.

– The army doesn't like more than one disaster in a day.
– Looks bad in the newspapers and upsets civilians at their breakfast.

I've killed women and children. I've killed everything that walks
or crawls at one time or another. And I'm here to kill you, Little Bill,
for what you done to Ned.

What I like and what I need are two different things.

Four dollars? You know what four dollars buys today?
It don't even buy three dollars!

– Have you read the Bible, Pete?
– Holy Bible?
– Yeah.
– Yeah, I think so. Anyway, I've heard about it.

## PLATOON  1986, USA
**Director:** Oliver Stone
**Cast:** Tom Berenger, Willem Dafoe, Charlie Sheen
**Screenplay:** Oliver Stone


## ZULU  1964, United Kingdom
**Director:** Cy Endfield
**Cast:** Stanley Baker, Jack Hawkins, Ulla Jacobsson
**Screenplay:** John Prebble and Cy Endfield

## UNFORGIVEN  1992, USA
**Director:** Clint Eastwood
**Cast:** Clint Eastwood, Gene Hackman, Morgan Freeman
**Screenplay:** David Webb Peoples

## THE WILD BUNCH  1969, USA
**Director:** Sam Peckinpah
**Cast:** William Holden, Ernest Borgnine, Robert Ryan
**Screenplay:** Walon Green, Roy N. Sickner and Sam Peckinpah

## SATURDAY NIGHT FEVER  1977, USA
**Director:** John Badham
**Cast:** John Travolta, Karen Lynn Gorney, Barry Miller
**Screenplay:** Nik Cohn and Norman Wexler

## BARTON FINK  1991, USA
**Director:** Joel Coen
**Cast:** John Turturro, John Goodman, Judy Davis
**Screenplay:** Ethan Coen and Joel Coen

– Money is the world's curse.
– May the Lord smite me with it!
And may I never recover!

Then one day I hear "Reach for it mister." I spun around, and there I was standing face to face with a six year old kid. Well, I just laid down my guns and walked away. Little bastard shot me in the ass!

– You got a letter from headquarters this morning.
– What is it?
– It's a big building where generals meet, but that's not important.

We are the Knights who say . . . NI!

You know, I got a hunch, Fat Man. I got a hunch that it's me from here on in. One ball, corner pocket. I mean, that ever happen to you? You know, all of a sudden you feel like you just can't miss? 'Cause I dreamed about this game, fat man. I dreamed about it every night on the road. Five ball. You know, this is my table, man. I own it.

– What do you want?
– Oh, little song, little dance, Batman's head on a lance.

## FIDDLER ON THE ROOF   1971, USA
**Director:** Norman Jewison
**Cast:** Topol, Norma Crane, Leonard Frey
**Screenplay:** Joseph Stein
*Based on the book by Sholom Aleichem*

## BLAZING SADDLES 1974, USA
**Director:** Mel Brooks
**Cast:** Cleavon Little, Gene Wilder, Harvey Korman
**Screenplay:** Andrew Bergman, Mel Brooks, Richard Pryor, Norman Steinberg
and Alan Uger

## AIRPLANE! / FLYING HIGH  1980, USA
**Director:** Jim Abrahams, David Zucker, Jerry Zucker
**Cast:** Robert Hays, Julie Hagerty, Robert Stack
**Screenplay:** Jim Abrahams, David Zucker and Jerry Zucker

## MONTY PYTHON AND THE HOLY GRAIL 1975, United Kingdom
**Director:** Terry Gilliam, Terry Jones
**Cast:** Graham Chapman, John Cleese, Terry Gilliam
**Screenplay:** Graham Chapman, John Cleese, Eric Idle, Terry Gilliam, Terry Jones
and Michael Palin

## THE HUSTLER 1961, USA
**Director:** Robert Rossen
**Cast:** Paul Newman, Jackie Gleason, Piper Laurie
**Screenplay:** Sidney Carroll and Robert Rossen
*Based on the book by Walter Tevis*

## BATMAN  1989, USA
**Director:** Tim Burton
**Cast:** Jack Nicholson, Michael Keaton, Kim Basinger
**Screenplay:** Bob Kane, Sam Hamm and Warren Skaaren

– Your middle name is Ralph, as in puke, your birthdate's
March 12th, you're 5'9 and a half, you weigh 130 pounds
and your social security number is 049380913.
– Wow! Are you psychic?
– No.
– Well, would you mind telling me how you know all this about me?
– I stole your wallet.

If you were happy every day of your life, you wouldn't be
a human being. You'd be a game-show host.

I'll send you a love letter! Straight from my heart, fucker!
You know what a love letter is? It's a bullet from a fucking gun,
fucker! You recieve a love letter from me, you're fucked forever!
You understand, fuck? I'll send you straight to hell, fucker!

A copper. A copper. How do you like that boys? A copper, and
his name is Fallon. And we went for it. I went for it. Treated him
like a kid brother. And I was gonna split fifty-fifty with a copper!

Well, I hope he likes spaghetti. They serve it four
times a day in Italian prisons!

Your car is uglier than I am. Oops, that didn't come out right.

## THE BREAKFAST CLUB 1985, USA
**Director:** John Hughes
**Cast:** Emilio Estevez, Judd Nelson, Molly Ringwald
**Screenplay:** John Hughes

## HEATHERS 1989, USA
**Director:** Michael Lehmann
**Cast:** Winona Ryder, Christian Slater, Shannen Doherty
**Screenplay:** Daniel Waters

## BLUE VELVET 1986, USA
**Director:** David Lynch
**Cast:** Kyle MacLachlan, Isabella Rossellini, Dennis Hopper
**Screenplay:** David Lynch

## WHITE HEAT 1949, USA
**Director:** Raoul Walsh
**Cast:** James Cagney, Virginia Mayo, Edmond O'Brien
**Screenplay:** Virginia Kellogg, Ivan Goff and Ben Roberts

## THE ITALIAN JOB 1969, United Kingdom
**Director:** Peter Collinson
**Cast:** Michael Caine, Noel Coward, Maggie Blye
**Screenplay:** Troy Kennedy-Martin

## AMERICAN GRAFFITI 1973, USA
**Director:** George Lucas
**Cast:** Richard Dreyfuss, Ron Howard, Paul Le Mat
**Screenplay:** George Lucas, Gloria Katz and Willard Huyck

– Is drinking a way of killing yourself?
– Or, is killing myself a way of drinking?

– All I know is that this violates every
canon of respectable broadcasting.
– We're not a respectable network. We're a whorehouse
network, and we have to take whatever we can get.

Hey, you wanna hear my philosophy of life? Do it to him
before he does it to you.

Our knowledge as made us cynical; our cleverness, hard
and unkind. We think too much and feel too little.

– This may seem like a really stupid question . . .
– There *are* no stupid questions.
– You inherit 5 million dollars the same day aliens land on the
earth and say they're going to blow it up in two days.
What do you do?
– That's the stupidest question I've ever heard.

## LEAVING LAS VEGAS 1995, USA
**Director:** Mike Figgis
**Cast:** Nicolas Cage, Elisabeth Shue, Julian Sands
**Screenplay:** Mike Figgis
*Based on the book by John O'Brien*

## NETWORK 1976, USA
**Director:** Sidney Lumet
**Cast:** William Holden, Faye Dunaway, Peter Finch
**Screenplay:** Paddy Chayefsky

## ON THE WATERFRONT 1954, USA
**Director:** Elia Kazan
**Cast:** Marlon Brando, Karl Malden, Rod Steiger
**Screenplay:** Bud Schulberg

## THE GREAT DICTATOR 1940, USA
**Director:** Charles Chaplin
**Cast:** Charles Chaplin, Jack Oakie, Reginald Gardiner
**Screenplay:** Charles Chaplin

## HEATHERS 1989, USA
**Director:** Michael Lehmann
**Cast:** Winona Ryder, Christian Slater, Shannen Doherty
**Screenplay:** Daniel Waters

They wanted in Hollywood to make the definitive spy picture. And they came to me to supervise the project, you know, because I think that, if you know me at all, you know that death is my bread and danger my butter—oh, no, danger's my bread, and death is my butter. No, no, wait. Danger's my bread, death no, death is—no, I'm sorry. Death is my—death and danger are my various breads and various butters.

I don't remember yesterday. Today it rained.

Muhammad Ali, he was like a sleeping elephant. You can do whatever you want around a sleeping elephant; whatever you want. But when he wakes up, he tramples everything.

Don't cry at the beginning of a date. Cry at the end, like I do.

He says the sun came out last night. He says it sang to him.

Aye, fight and you may die, run and you'll live, at least a while. And ... dying in your beds, many years from now, would you be willin to trade all the days, from this day to that, for one chance, just one chance, to come back here and tell our enemies that they may take our lives, but they'll never take ... OUR FREEDOM!

## WHAT'S UP, TIGER LILY? 1966, Japan
**Director:** Senkichi Taniguchi
**Cast:** Tatsuya Mihashi, Mie Hama, Akiko Wakabayashi
**Screenplay:** Woody Allen, Julie Bennett, Frank Buxton, Louise Lasser, Len Maxwell, Mickey Rose and Bryan Wilson

## THREE DAYS OF THE CONDOR 1975, USA
**Director:** Sydney Pollack
**Cast:** Robert Redford, Faye Dunaway, Cliff Robertson
**Screenplay:** Lorenzo Semple Jr. and David Rayfiel
*Based on the book by James Grady*

## WHEN WE WERE KINGS 1996, USA
**Director:** Leon Gast
**Cast:** Muhammad Ali, George Foreman, Don King

## JERRY MAGUIRE 1996, USA
**Director:** Cameron Crowe
**Cast:** Tom Cruise, Cuba Gooding Jr., Renee Zellweger
**Screenplay:** Cameron Crowe

## CLOSE ENCOUNTERS OF THE THIRD KIND 1977, USA
**Director:** Steven Spielberg
**Cast:** Richard Dreyfuss, François Truffaut, Teri Garr
**Screenplay:** Steven Spielberg, Hal Barwood, Jerry Belson, John Hill and Matthew Robbins

## BRAVEHEART 1995, USA
**Director:** Mel Gibson
**Cast:** Mel Gibson, Sophie Marceau, Patrick McGoohan
**Screenplay:** Randall Wallace

I don't feel the sickness yet, but it's in the post. That's for sure. I'm in the junkie limbo at the moment. Too ill to sleep. Too tired to stay awake, but the sickness is on its way. Sweat, chills, nausea. Pain and craving. A need like nothing else I've ever known will soon take hold of me. It's on its way.

Even a stopped clock tells the right time twice a day, and for once I'm inclined to believe Withnail is right. We are indeed drifting into the arena of the unwell.

– Sir, could I please see your license?
– Whuut?
– Your license. Where's your license?
– It's back there on the bumper, man!

He who draws the sword from the stone, he shall be king. Arthur, you're the one!

– How did you know? How did you know I'd respond to you the way I have?
– I saw myself in you.

If anything in this life is certain, if history has taught us anything, it is that you can kill anyone.

## TRAINSPOTTING 1996, United Kingdom
**Director:** Danny Boyle
**Cast:** Ewan McGregor, Ewan Bremmer, Jonny Lee Miller
**Screenplay:** John Hodge
*Based on the book by Irvine Welsh*


## WITHNAIL AND I 1987, USA
**Director:** Bruce Robinson
**Cast:** Richard E. Grant, Paul McGann, Richard Griffiths
**Screenplay:** Bruce Robinson


## UP IN SMOKE 1978, USA
**Director:** Lou Adler
**Cast:** Cheech Marin, Tommy Chong, Stacy Keach
**Screenplay:** Tommy Chong and Cheech Marin


## EXCALIBUR 1991, USA
**Director:** John Boorman
**Cast:** Nicol Williamson, Nigel Terry, Helen Mirren
**Screenplay:** Rospo Pallenberg and John Boorman
*Based on the book by Sir Thomas Malory*


## 9 1/2 WEEKS 1986, USA
**Director:** Adrian Lyne
**Cast:** Mickey Rourke, Kim Basinger, Margaret Whitton
**Screenplay:** Sarah Kernochan, Zalman King, Patricia Louisianna Knop
*Based on the book by Elizabeth McNeill*


## THE GODFATHER PART II 1974, USA
**Director:** Francis Ford Coppola
**Cast:** Al Pacino, Robert De Niro, Robert Duvall
**Screenplay:** Mario Puzo and Francis Ford Coppola

You know, we always called each other goodfellas. Like, you'd say to somebody: You're gonna like this guy; he's all right. He's a goodfella. He's one of us. You understand? We were goodfellas, wiseguys.

You see, I have a story too, Mr. Bailey. I had a friend once. A dear friend. I turned him in to save his life. He died. But he wanted it that way. Things went bad for my friend, and they went bad for me too.

You wanna fuck with me? Okay. You wanna play rough? Okay. Say hello to my little friend.

– Are you afraid to die, Spartacus?
– No more than I was to be born.

– Well, Denham, the airplanes got him.
– Oh, no. It wasn't the airplanes. It was beauty killed the beast.

Ray, people will come, Ray. They'll come to Iowa for reasons they can't even fathom. They'll turn up your driveway, not knowing for sure why they're doing it. They'll arrive at your door as innocent as children, longing for the past . . .

## GOODFELLAS 1990, USA

**Director:** Martin Scorsese
**Cast:** Robert De Niro, Ray Liotta, Joe Pesci
**Screenplay:** Nicholas Pileggi and Martin Scorsese
*Based on the book by Nicholas Pileggi*

## ONCE UPON A TIME IN AMERICA 1984, USA

**Director:** Sergio Leone
**Cast:** Robert De Niro, James Woods, Elizabeth McGovern
**Screenplay:** Leonardo Benvenuti, Piero De Bernardi, Enrico Medioli, Franco Arcalli, Franco Ferrini, Sergio Leone, Stuart Kaminsky and Ernesto Gastaldi
*Based on the book by Harry Grey*

## SCARFACE 1983, USA

**Director:** Brian De Palma
**Cast:** Al Pacino, Steven Bauer, Michelle Pfeiffer
**Screenplay:** Oliver Stone and Howard Hawks *Based on the book by Armitage Trail*

## SPARTACUS 1960, USA

**Director:** Stanley Kubrick
**Cast:** Kirk Douglas, Laurence Olivier, Jean Simmons
**Screenplay:** Dalton Trumbo, Calder Willingham and Peter Ustinov
*Based on the book by Howard Fast*

## KING KONG 1933, USA

**Directors:** Merian C. Cooper, Ernest B. Schoedsack
**Cast:** Fay Wray, Robert Armstrong and Bruce Cabot
**Screenplay:** James Ashmore Creelman and Ruth Rose

## FIELD OF DREAMS 1989, USA

**Director:** Phil Alden Robinson
**Cast:** Kevin Costner, Amy Madigan, Gaby Hoffmann
**Screenplay:** Phil Alden Robinson *Based on the book by W.P. Kinsella*

I hope they don't hang you, Precious, by that sweet neck.
Yes, angel, I'm gonna send you over. The chances are you'll get off
with life. That means if you're a good girl, you'll be out in twenty years.
I'll be waiting for you. If they hang you, I'll always remember you.


. . . Inside the Ark are treasures beyond your wildest aspirations.
You want to see it opened as well as I. Indiana, we are simply
passing through history. This, this is history.


I'm tired, I've been drinking since nine o'clock. My wife is
vomiting. There's been a lot of screaming going on around here!


We were attracted to each other at the party. That was obvious!
You're on your own for the night, that's also obvious . . .
We're two adults.


Well, this is not a boat accident! And it wasn't any propeller; and it
wasn't any coral reef, and it wasn't Jack the Ripper. It was a shark.


– DO YOU SEE THE LIGHT?
– THE BAND!
– DO YOU SEE THE LIGHT?
– What light?
– HAVE YOU SEEEEN THE LIGHT?
– YES! YES! JESUS H. TAP-DANCING CHRIST
. . . I HAVE SEEN THE LIGHT!

## THE MALTESE FALCON 1941, USA
**Director:** John Huston
**Cast:** Humphrey Bogart, Mary Astor, Peter Lorre
**Screenplay:** John Huston
*Based on the book by Dashiell Hammett*

## RAIDERS OF THE LOST ARK 1981, USA
**Director:** Steven Spielberg
**Cast:** Harrison Ford, Karen Allen, Wolf Kahler
**Screenplay:** George Lucas, Philip Kaufman and Lawrence Kasdan

## WHO'S AFRAID OF VIRGINIA WOOLF 1966, USA
**Director:** Mike Nichols  **Cast:** Elizabeth Taylor, Richard Burton, George Segal
**Screenplay:** Edward Albee and Ernest Lehman

## FATAL ATTRACTION 1987, USA
**Director:** Adrian Lyne
**Cast:** Michael Douglas, Glenn Close, Anne Archer
**Screenplay:** James Dearden and Nicholas Meyer

## JAWS 1975, USA
**Director:** Steven Spielberg
**Cast:** Roy Scheider, Robert Shaw, Richard Dreyfuss
**Screenplay:** Peter Benchley, Carl Gottlieb, John Milius, Howard Sackler
    and Robert Shaw *Based on the book by Peter Benchley*

## THE BLUES BROTHERS 1980, USA
**Director:** John Landis
**Cast:** John Belushi, Dan Aykroyd, Cab Calloway
**Screenplay:** Dan Aykroyd and John Landis

– Ya know, you see a girl a couple of times a week, just for laughs, and right away they think you're gonna divorce your wife. Now I ask you, is that fair?
– No, sir, it's very unfair. Especially to your wife.


– Crucifixion?
– Yes.
– Good. Out of the door, line on the left, one cross each.
– Crucifixion?
– Er, no. Freedom, actually.
– What?
– Yeah, they said I hadn't done anything and I could go and live on an island somewhere.
– Oh, I say! That's very nice. Well, off you go then.
– No, I'm just pulling your leg, it's crucifixion really.
– Oh yes, very good. Well . . .
– Yes, I know. Out of the door, one cross each, line on the left.


You see, Mr. Scott? In the water, I'm a very skinny lady!


You know those days when you get the mean reds?


Flowers are essentially tarts; prostitutes for the bees.


– Where ya from, man?
– Hard to say.

## THE APARTMENT 1960, USA
**Director:** Billy Wilder **Cast:** Jack Lemmon, Shirley MacLaine, Fred MacMurray
**Screenplay:** Billy Wilder and I.A.L. Diamond

## MONTY PYTHON'S LIFE OF BRIAN 1979, United Kingdom
**Director:** Terry Jones
**Cast:** Graham Chapman, John Cleese, Terry Gilliam
**Screenplay:** Graham Chapman, John Cleese, Terry Gilliam, Eric Idle, Terry Jones
and Michael Palin

## THE POSEIDON ADVENTURE 1972, USA
**Director:** Ronald Neame **Cast:** Gene Hackman, Ernest Borgnine, Red Buttons
**Screenplay:** Wendell Mayes and Stirling Silliphant *Based on the book by Paul Gallico*

## BREAKFAST AT TIFFANY'S 1961, USA
**Director:** Blake Edwards **Cast:** Audrey Hepburn, George Peppard
**Screenplay:** Truman Capote, George Axelrod

## WITHNAIL AND I 1985, USA
**Director:** Bruce Robinson **Cast:** Richard E. Grant, Paul McGann, Richard Griffiths
**Screenplay:** Bruce Robinson

## EASY RIDER 1969, USA
**Director:** Dennis Hopper **Cast:** Peter Fonda, Dennis Hopper, Jack Nicholson
**Screenplay:** Peter Fonda, Dennis Hopper and Terry Southern

– Jesus, Bob. You never told us anything about not mentioning dogs.
– The reason nobody mentioned dogs, Rick, is that to
mention the dog would have been a hex in itself.
– All right. Well, now we are on the subject, are there an other stupid
things we aren't supposed to mention that will affect our future?

Lower your flags, and march straight back to England, stopping
at every home to beg forgiveness for a hundred years of theft,
rape, and murder. Do this, and your men shall live. Do it not,
and every one of you will die today.

It happens sometimes. People just explode. Natural causes.

You know, I'd almost forgotten what your eyes looked like.
Still the same. Pissholes in the snow.

You can get further with a kind word and a gun than you
can with just a kind word.

– It's when you start doing things for free,
that you start to grow wings. Isn't that right, Mike?
– What?
– Wings, Michael. You grow wings, and become a fairy.

## DRUGSTORE COWBOY 1989, USA
**Director:** Gus Van Sant
**Cast:** Matt Dillon, Kelly Lynch, James Remar
**Screenplay:** Gus Van Sant, Daniel Yost and William S. Burroughs
*Based on the book by James Fogle*

## BRAVEHEART 1995, USA
**Director:** Mel Gibson
**Cast:** Mel Gibson, Sophie Marceau, Patrick McGoohan
**Screenplay:** Randall Wallace

## REPO MAN 1984, USA
**Director:** Alex Cox
**Cast:** Emilio Estevez, Harry Dean Stanton, Vonetta McGee
**Screenplay:** Alex Cox

## GET CARTER 1971, United Kingdom
**Director:** Mike Hodges
**Cast:** Michael Caine, Ian Hendry, Britt Ekland
**Screenplay:** Mike Hodges
*Based on the book by Ted Lewis*

## THE UNTOUCHABLES 1987, USA
**Director:** Brian De Palma
**Cast:** Kevin Costner, Sean Connery, Charles Martin Smith
**Screenplay:** David Mamet
*Based on the book by Oscar Fraley and Eliot Ness and Paul Robsky*

## MY OWN PRIVATE IDAHO 1991, USA
**Director:** Gus Van Sant
**Cast:** River Phoenix, Keanu Reeves, James Russo
**Screenplay:** Gus Van Sant

– Do you feel that playing rock 'n' roll music keeps you a child? That is, keeps you in a state of arrested development?
– No. No. No. I feel it's like, it's more like going, going to a, a national park or something. And there's, you know, they preserve the moose. And that's, that's my childhood up there on stage. That moose, you know.
– So when you're playing you feel like a preserved moose on stage?
– Yeah.

– Have you been following that man?
– Yeah, I've been following him on my own time. And anybody can tell I didn't do that to him.
– How?
– Cause he looks too damn good, that's how!

Six days does not a week make.

It's important to think. It's what separates us from lentils.

Paulie might have moved slow, but it was only because Paulie didn't have to move for anybody.

## THIS IS SPINAL TAP 1984, USA
**Director:** Rob Reiner
**Cast:** Michael McKean, Christopher Guest, Harry Shearer
**Screenplay:** Christopher Guest, Michael McKean, Rob Reiner and Harry Shearer

## DIRTY HARRY 1971, USA
**Director:** Don Siegal
**Cast:** Clint Eastwood, Harry Guardino, Reni Santoni
**Screenplay:** Harry Julian Fink, Rita M. Fink, Dean Riesner and John Milius

## BAREFOOT IN THE PARK 1967, USA
**Director:** Gene Saks
**Cast:** Robert Redford, Jane Fonda, Charles Boyer
**Screenplay:** Neil Simon

## THE FISHER KING 1991, USA
**Director:** Terry Gilliam
**Cast:** Robin Williams, Jeff Bridges, Amanda Plummer
**Screenplay:** Richard LaGravenese

## GOODFELLAS 1990, USA
**Director:** Martin Scorsese
**Cast:** Robert De Niro, Ray Liotta, Joe Pesci
**Screenplay:** Nicholas Pileggi and Martin Scorsese
*Based on the book by Nicholas Pileggi*

It has been established that persons who have recently died
have been returning to life and committing acts of murder . . .

– We're here to meet a friend. Comin' on the train.
– Nothin' comin' on the train except a couple
of crates and a . . . uh . . . coffin!
– Our friend.

Last night, Darth Vader came down from planet Vulcan and
told me that if I didn't take Lorraine out that he'd melt my brain.

Nicky's methods of betting weren't scientific, but they worked.
When he won, he collected. When he lost, he told the bookies to
go fuck themselves. I mean, what were they going to do, muscle
Nicky? Nicky was the muscle.

I must be crazy to be in a loony bin like this.

I done something new for this fight! I done wrestled with a
alligator! That's right, I have rassled with a alligator. I done tussled
with a whale! I done handcuffed lightning, throwed thunder in jail!
That's bad. Only last week, I murdered a rock, injured a stone,
hospitalized a brick. I'm so mean, I make medicine sick!

## NIGHT OF THE LIVING DEAD  1968, USA
**Director:** George A. Romero
**Cast:** Duane Jones, Judith O'Dea
**Screenplay:** George A. Romero and John A. Russo

## MAD MAX  1979, Australia
**Director:** George Miller
**Cast:** Mel Gibson, Joanne Samuel, Hugh Keays Byrne
**Screenplay:** James McCausland and George Miller

## BACK TO THE FUTURE  1985, USA
**Director:** Robert Zemeckis
**Cast:** Michael J. Fox, Christopher Lloyd, Crispin Glover
**Screenplay:** Robert Zemeckis and Bob Gale

## CASINO  1995, USA
**Director:** Martin Scorsese
**Cast:** Robert De Niro, Sharon Stone, Joe Pesci
**Screenplay:** Nicholas Pileggi and Martin Scorsese
*Based on the book by Nicholas Pileggi*

## ONE FLEW OVER THE CUCKOO'S NEST  1975, USA
**Director:** Milos Forman
**Cast:** Jack Nicholson, Louise Fletcher, Brad Dourif
**Screenplay:** Bo Goldman and Lawrence Hauben
*Based on the book by Ken Kesey*

## WHEN WE WERE KINGS  1996, USA
**Director:** Leon Gast
**Cast:** Muhammad Ali, George Foreman, Don King

– D'you know that the human head weighs 8 pounds?
– Did you know that Troy Aikman, in only six years,
has passed for 16,303 yards?
– D'you know that bees and dogs can smell fear?
– Did you know that the career record for hits is 4,256 by Pete Rose
who is NOT in the Hall of Fame?
– D'you know that my next door neighbor has three rabbits?
– I . . . I can't compete with that!

I don't think I want to know you very well. I don't think
you're gonna live much longer.

Tell me something, my friend. Have you ever danced with the devil
by the pale moonlight?

You wouldn't hit a man with no
trousers on would you?

Have you had a close encounter?

## JERRY MAGUIRE 1996, USA
**Director:** Cameron Crowe
**Cast:** Tom Cruise, Cuba Gooding Jr., Renee Zellweger
**Screenplay:** Cameron Crowe

## THREE DAYS OF THE CONDOR 1975, USA
**Director:** Sydney Pollack
**Cast:** Robert Redford, Faye Dunaway, Cliff Robertson
**Screenplay:** Lorenzo Semple Jr. and David Rayfiel
*Based on the book by James Grady*

## BATMAN 1989, USA
**Director:** Tim Burton
**Cast:** Jack Nicholson, Michael Keaton, Kim Basinger
**Screenplay:** Bob Kane, Sam Hamm and Warren Skaaren

## THE ITALIAN JOB 1969, United Kingdom
**Director:** Peter Collinson
**Cast:** Michael Caine, Noel Coward, Maggie Blye
**Screenplay:** Troy Kennedy-Martin

## CLOSE ENCOUNTERS OF THE THIRD KIND 1977, USA
**Director:** Steven Spielberg
**Cast:** Richard Dreyfuss, François Truffaut, Teri Garr
**Screenplay:** Steven Spielberg, Hal Barwood, Jerry Belson, John Hill
and Matthew Robbins

The soul of man has been given wings and at last he is beginning to fly. He is flying into the rainbow! Into the light of hope, into the future!

Impressive. Most impressive. Obi-wan has taught you well. You have controlled your fear. Now, release your anger! Only your hatred can destroy me!

Now you listen to me, I'm an advertising man, not a red herring. I've got a job, a secretary, a mother, two ex-wives and several bartenders that depend upon me, and I don't intend to disappoint them all by getting myself "slightly" killed.

– What happened to your nose, Gittes? Somebody slammed a bedroom window on it? – Nope. Your wife got excited. She crossed her legs a little too quick. You understand what I mean, pal?

– Yessir. J.W., let me have a word with ya. J.W., now this fellow's from London England. He's a Englishman workin' in cooperation with our boys, a sorta . . . secret agent. – Secret Agent? On whose side?

## THE GREAT DICTATOR 1940, USA
**Director:** Charles Chaplin
**Cast:** Charles Chaplin, Jack Oakie, Reginald Gardiner
**Screenplay:** Charles Chaplin

## THE EMPIRE STRIKES BACK 1980, USA
**Director:** Irwin Kershner
**Cast:** Mark Hamill, Harrison Ford, Carrie Fisher
**Screenplay:** George Lucas, Leigh Brackett and Lawrence Kasdan

## NORTH BY NORTHWEST 1959, USA
**Director:** Alfred Hitchcock
**Cast:** Cary Grant, Eva Marie Saint, James Mason
**Screenplay:** Ernest Lehman

## CHINATOWN 1974, USA
**Director:** Roman Polanski
**Cast:** Jack Nicholson, Faye Dunaway, John Huston
**Screenplay:** Robert Towne and Roman Polanski

## LIVE AND LET DIE 1973, United Kingdom
**Director:** Guy Hamilton
**Cast:** Roger Moore, Yaphet Kotto, Jane Seymour
**Screenplay:** Tom Mankiewicz
*Based on the book by Ian Fleming*

A census taker once tried to test me. I ate his liver
with some fava beans and a nice Chianti.

You make it with some of these chicks, they
think you gotta dance with them.

– Well, I guess he had it comin'.
– We all got it comin' kid.

– There's something I've been meaning to ask you for some time now.
– What's that?
– Can you cure me?
– No. We can care for you, but we can't cure you.

I find it difficult to convince myself that God would have
introduced such a foul being into creation without endowing
her with some virtues, hmmm?

## THE SILENCE OF THE LAMBS 1991, USA
**Director:** Jonathan Demme
**Cast:** Jodie Foster, Anthony Hopkins, Scott Glenn
**Screenplay:** Ted Tally
*Based on the book by Thomas Harris*

## SATURDAY NIGHT FEVER 1977, USA
**Director:** John Badham
**Cast:** John Travolta, Karen Lynn Gorney, Barry Miller
**Screenplay:** Nik Cohn and Norman Wexler

## UNFORGIVEN 1992, USA
**Director:** Clint Eastwood
**Cast:** Clint Eastwood, Gene Hackman, Morgan Freeman
**Screenplay:** David Webb Peoples

## THE ELEPHANT MAN 1980, USA
**Director:** David Lynch
**Cast:** Anthony Hopkins, John Hurt, Anne Bancroft
**Screenplay:** Christopher De Vore, Eric Bergren and David Lynch
*Based on the book by Sir Frederick Treves and Ashley Montagu*

## THE NAME OF THE ROSE 1986, Frane/Italy/West Germany
**Director:** Jean Jacques Annaud
**Cast:** Sean Connery, F. Murray Abraham, Christian Slater
**Screenplay:** Andrew Birkin, Gérard Brach, Howard Franklin and Alain Godard
*Based on the book by Umberto Eco*

– Hold on to yourself, Bartlett. You're twenty feet short.
– What do you mean, twenty feet short?
– You're twenty feet short of the woods. The hole is right here out in open. The guard is between us and the lights.

– When I get out, you're dead!
– You might be dead before you get out.

Short people have long faces and long people have short faces. Big people have little humor, and little people have no humor at all.

I thrill when I drill a bicuspid / It's swell though they tell me I'm mal-ad-just-ed.

When it comes to the safety of these people, there's me and then there's God, understand?

– Wait a minute, Doc. Ah . . . Are you telling me you built a time machine . . . out of a DeLorean?
– The way I see it, if you're gonna build a time machine into a car, why not do it with some style?

## THE GREAT ESCAPE 1963, USA
**Director:** John Sturges
**Cast:** Steve McQueen, James Garner, Richard Attenborough
**Screenplay:** James Clavell and W.R. Burnett
*Based on the book by Paul Brickhill*

## ESCAPE FROM ALCATRAZ 1979, USA
**Director:** Donald Siegel
**Cast:** Clint Eastwood, Patrick McGoohan, Roberts Blossom
**Screenplay:** Richard Tuggle
*Based on the book by J. Campbell Bruce*

## SINGIN' IN THE RAIN 1952, USA
**Director:** Gene Kelly, Stanley Donen
**Cast:** Gene Kelly, Debbie Reynolds, Donald O'Connor
**Screenplay:** Betty Comden and Adolph Green

## LITTLE SHOP OF HORRORS 1986, USA
**Director:** Frank Oz
**Cast:** Rick Moranis, Ellen Greene, Vincent Gardenia
**Screenplay:** Charles B. Griffith and Howard Ashman

## THE ABYSS 1989, USA
**Director:** James Cameron
**Cast:** Ed Harris, Mary Elizabeth Mastrantonio, Michael Biehn
**Screenplay:** James Cameron

## BACK TO THE FUTURE 1985, USA
**Director:** Robert Zemeckis
**Cast:** Michael J. Fox, Christopher Lloyd, Crispin Glover
**Screenplay:** Robert Zemeckis and Bob Gale

Why have you disturbed our sleep? Awakened us from our
ancient slumber? YOU WILL DIE ...

You know what you done there? You told my story. You told
my whole story right there, right there. One time, I told you I was
gonna make you somebody. That's what you done for me. You
made me somebody they're gonna remember.

Any time you try a decent crime, you got fifty ways you're gonna
fuck up. If you think of twenty-five of them, then you're a genius
... and you ain't no genius. You remember who told me that?

Ollie, you know my feelings about arming morons: you arm one,
you've got to arm them all, otherwise it wouldn't be good sport.

I move around a lot. Not because I'm looking for anything really,
but 'cause I'm getting away from things that get bad if I stay.

I run my unit how I run my unit. You want to investigate me? Roll
the dice and take your chances. I eat breakfast 300 yards from 4,000
Cubans who are trained to kill me, so don't think for one second that
you can come down here, flash a badge, and make me nervous.

## THE EVIL DEAD 1983, USA
**Director:** Sam Raimi
**Cast:** Bruce Campbell, Ellen Sandweiss
**Screenplay:** Sam Raimi

## BONNIE AND CLYDE 1967, USA
**Director:** Arthur Penn
**Cast:** Warren Beatty, Faye Dunaway, Michael J. Pollard
**Screenplay:** David Newman (III), Robert Benton and Robert Towne

## BODY HEAT 1981, USA
**Director:** Lawrence Kasdan
**Cast:** William Hurt, Kathleen Turner, Richard Crenna
**Screenplay:** Lawrence Kasdan

## NOBODY'S FOOL 1994, USA
**Director:** Robert Benton
**Cast:** Paul Newman, Jessica Tandy, Bruce Willis
**Screenplay:** Robert Benton
*Based on the book by Richard Russo*

## FIVE EASY PIECES 1970, USA
**Director:** Bob Rafelson
**Cast:** Jack Nicholson, Karen Black, Billy Green Bush
**Screenplay:** Carole Eastman and Bob Rafelson

## A FEW GOOD MEN 1992, USA
**Director:** Rob Reiner
**Cast:** Tom Cruise, Jack Nicholson, Demi Moore
**Screenplay:** Aaron Sorkin

I remember when my daddy gave me that gun. He told me that I should never point it at anything in the house; and that he'd rather I'd shoot at tin cans in the backyard. But he said that sooner or later he supposed the temptation to go after birds would be too much, and that I could shoot all the blue jays I wanted—if I could hit 'em, but to remember it was a sin to kill a mockingbird. Well, I reckon because mockingbirds don't do anything but make music for us to enjoy . . .

– Never trust a nigger.
– He could have been white.
– Never trust anyone!

– I saw Alan this morning and you know what I can't figure out?
– Alan's in Utah.
– I . . . can't figure out what I was doing in Utah this morning.

– What are some of your favorite things to do?
– Well, on Sundays I used to like to go hiking, but now . . .

I would like, if I may, to take you on a strange journey.

## TO KILL A MOCKINGBIRD 1962, USA
**Director:** Robert Mulligan
**Cast:** Gregory Peck, Mary Badham, Philip Alford
**Screenplay:** Horton Foote
*Based on the book by Harper Lee*

## THE FRENCH CONNECTION 1971, USA
**Director:** William Friedkin
**Cast:** Gene Hackman, Fernando Rey, Roy Scheider
**Screenplay:** Ernest Tidyman, Edward M. Keyes
*Based on the book by Robin Moore*

## FLETCH 1985, USA
**Director:** Michael Ritchie
**Cast:** Chevy Chase, Dana Wheeler Nicholson, Tim Matheson
**Screenplay:** Andrew Bergman
*Based on the book by Gregory McDonald*

## THE BLAIR WITCH PROJECT 1999, USA
**Director:** Daniel Myrick, Eduardo Sánchez
**Cast:** Heather Donahue, Joshua Leonard, Michael C. Williams
**Screenplay:** Daniel Myrick, Eduardo Sánchez

## THE ROCKY HORROR PICTURE SHOW 1975, USA
**Director:** Jim Sharman
**Cast:** Tim Curry, Susan Sarandon, Barry Bostwick
**Screenplay:** Richard O'Brien, Jim Sharman

– Splendid, I thought. What did you think?
– I, thought, splendid! What did you think?
– Splendid, I thought.

You still don't know what you're dealing with, do you? Perfect organism.
Its structural perfection is matched only by its hostility.

. . . If I ever lay my two eyes on you again, I'm gonna
walk right up to you and hammer on that monkeyed
skull of yours 'til it rings like a Chinese gong!

In the year of our Lord thirteen fourteen, patriots of Scotland,
starving and outnumbered, charged the fields of Bannockburn.
They fought like warrior poets. They fought like Scotsmen.
And won their freedom.

As far back as I can remember,
I always wanted to be a gangster.

– I know you better than you know yourself.
– You never had a camera in my head.

## FOUR WEDDINGS AND A FUNERAL 1994, United Kingdom
**Director:** Mike Newell
**Cast:** Hugh Grant, Andie MacDowell, Kristin Scott Thomas
**Screenplay:** Richard Curtis

## ALIEN 1979, USA
**Director:** Ridley Scott
**Cast:** Tom Skerritt, Sigourney Weaver, John Hurt
**Screenplay:** Dan O'Bannon, Ronald Shusett, Dan O'Bannon, David Giler
and Walter Hill

## HIS GIRL FRIDAY 1940, USA
**Director:** Howard Hawks
**Cast:** Cary Grant, Rosalind Russell, Ralph Bellamy
**Screenplay:** Ben Hecht, Charles MacArthur and Charles Lederer

## BRAVEHEART 1995, USA
**Director:** Mel Gibson
**Cast:** Mel Gibson, Sophie Marceau, Patrick McGoohan
**Screenplay:** Randall Wallace

## GOODFELLAS 1990, USA
**Director:** Martin Scorsese
**Cast:** Robert De Niro, Ray Liotta, Joe Pesci
**Screenplay:** Nicholas Pileggi and Martin Scorsese
*Based on the book by Nicholas Pileggi*

## THE TRUMAN SHOW 1998, USA
**Director:** Peter Weir
**Cast:** Jim Carrey, Laura Linney, Ed Harris
**Screenplay:** Andrew Niccol

Well it's not a train. It's a prison word for . . . escape.
But it doesn't stop around here.

– Well, what are you going to do now? Shoot me?
– No, I don't think so.
– Then you're going to take these from me? If I could say a
word about that . . .
– No, you can keep them. You can keep as many as you can swallow.

Thank God for the rain, to wash the trash off the sidewalk.

Ya smoke this shit so's to escape from reality?
Me, I don't need this shit. I am reality.
There's the way it ought to be, and there's the way it is.

I gotta tell you . . . the life of the mind . . . There's no
road map for that territory . . .
And exploring it can be painful.

Protecting the Queen's safety is a task that is gladly accepted by
Police Squad. No matter how silly the idea of having a queen might
be to us, as Americans we must be gracious and considerate hosts.

## MIDNIGHT EXPRESS 1978, USA
**Director:** Alan Parker
**Cast:** Brad Davis, Irene Miracle, Bo Hopkins
**Screenplay:** Oliver Stone
*Based on the book by Billy Hayes and William Hoffer*

## MARATHON MAN 1976, USA
**Director:** John Schlesinger
**Cast:** Dustin Hoffman, Laurence Olivier, Roy Scheider
**Screenplay:** William Goldman
*Based on the book by William Goldman*

## TAXI DRIVER 1976, USA
**Director:** Martin Scorsese
**Cast:** Robert De Niro, Cybill Shepherd, Harvey Keitel
**Screenplay:** Paul Schrader

## PLATOON 1986, USA
**Director:** Oliver Stone
**Cast:** Tom Berenger, Willem Dafoe, Charlie Sheen
**Screenplay:** Oliver Stone

## BARTON FINK 1991, USA
**Director:** Joel Coen
**Cast:** John Turturro, John Goodman, Judy Davis
**Screenplay:** Ethan Coen and Joel Coen

## THE NAKED GUN: FROM THE FILES OF POLICE SQUAD 1988, USA
**Director:** David Zucker
**Cast:** Leslie Nielsen, George Kennedy, Priscilla Presley
**Screenplay:** Jim Abrahams, David Zucker and Pat Proft

Oh! They've encased him in Carbonite! He should be quite well protected. If he survived the freezing process, that is.

– Hi, I'm Diana Christensen, a racist lackey
of the imperialist ruling circles.
– Laureen Hobbs, badass commie nigger.

They're not that different from you, are they? Same haircuts. Full of hormones, just like you. Invincible, just like you feel. The world is their oyster. They believe they're destined for great things, just like many of you, their eyes are full of hope, just like you. Did they wait until it was too late to make from their lives even one iota of what they were capable? Because, you see, gentlemen, these boys are now fertilizing daffodils. But if you listen real close, you can hear them whisper their legacy to you.

You are certainly the most distinguished group of highway scofflaws and degenerates ever gathered together in one place.

– You know, the one thing I can't figure out.
Are these girls real smart or real real lucky?
– Don't matter. Brains'll only get you so far
and luck always runs out.

## THE EMPIRE STRIKES BACK 1980, USA
**Director:** Irwin Kershner
**Cast:** Mark Hamill, Harrison Ford, Carrie Fisher
**Screenplay:** George Lucas, Leigh Brackett and Lawrence Kasdan

## NETWORK 1976, USA
**Director:** Sidney Lumet
**Cast:** William Holden, Faye Dunaway, Peter Finch
**Screenplay:** Paddy Chayefsky

## DEAD POETS SOCIETY 1989, USA
**Director:** Peter Weir
**Cast:** Robin Williams, Robert Sean Leonard, Ethan Hawke
**Screenplay:** Tom Schulman

## THE CANNONBALL RUN 1981, USA
**Director:** Hal Needham
**Cast:** Burt Reynolds, Roger Moore, Farrah Fawcett
**Screenplay:** Brock Yates

## THELMA & LOUISE 1991, USA
**Director:** Ridley Scott
**Cast:** Susan Sarandon, Geena Davis, Harvey Keitel
**Screenplay:** Callie Khouri

If you want me to keep my mouth shut, it's gonna cost you some dough. I figure a thousand bucks is reasonable, so I want two.

The city is made of bricks. The strong make many, the starving make few, the dead make none. So much for accusations.

. . . I am the rocker, I am the roller, I am the out-of-controller!

– Lobotomy? Isn't that for loonies?
– Not at all. Friend of mine had one. Designer of the neutron bomb. You ever hear of the neutron bomb? Destroys people—leaves buildings standing. Fits in a suitcase. It's so small, no one knows it's there until—BLAMMO! Eyes melt, skin explodes, everybody dead! So immoral, working on the thing can drive you mad. That's what happened to this friend of mine. So he had a lobotomy. Now he's well again.

I don't think I've ever drunk champagne before breakfast before. With breakfast on several occasions, but never before, before.

– God is on our side because he hates the Yanks!
– God is not on our side because he hates idiots also.

## MILLER'S CROSSING 1990, USA
**Director:** Joel Coen
**Cast:** Gabriel Byrne, Albert Finney, Marcia Gay Harden
**Screenplay:** Joel Coen and Ethan Coen *Based on the book by Dashiell Hammett*

## THE TEN COMMANDMENTS 1956, USA
**Director:** Cecil B. DeMille
**Cast:** Charlton Heston, Yul Brynner, Anne Baxter
**Screenplay:** J.H. Ingraham, A.E. Southon, Dorothy Clarke Wilson,
Æneas MacKenzie, Jesse Lasky Jr., Jack Gariss and Fredric M. Frank.

## MAD MAX 1979, Australia
**Director:** George Miller
**Cast:** Mel Gibson, Joanne Samuel, Hugh Keays Byrne
**Screenplay:** James McCausland and George Miller

## REPO MAN 1984, USA
**Director:** Alex Cox
**Cast:** Emilio Estevez, Harry Dean Stanton, Vonetta McGee
**Screenplay:** Alex Cox

## BREAKFAST AT TIFFANY'S 1961, USA
**Director:** Blake Edwards
**Cast:** Audrey Hepburn, George Peppard
**Screenplay:** Truman Capote, George Axelrod

## THE GOOD, THE BAD, AND THE UGLY 1966, Italy
**Director:** Sergio Leone
**Cast:** Clint Eastwood, Lee Van Cleef, Eli Wallach
**Screenplay:** Luciano Vincenzoni, Sergio Leone, Agenore Incrocci and Furio Scarpelli

It was one of those days when it's a minute away from snowing and there's this electricity in the air. You can almost hear it. And this bag was, like, dancing with me. Like a little kid begging me to play with it. For fifteen minutes. And that's the day I knew there was this entire life behind things, and . . . this incredibly benevolent force, that wanted me to know there was no reason to be afraid, ever. Video's a poor excuse. But it helps me remember . . . and I need to remember. Sometimes, there's so much beauty in the world I feel like I can't take it, like my heart's going to cave in.

You have broken what could not be broken! Now, hope is broken.

– I want to know more about you.
– You already know enough about me. Any more and you're going to get a headache.

When they send for you, you go in alive, you come out dead, and it's your best friend that does it.

I think I must have one of those faces you can't help believing.

It's not you marrying me. It's me marrying anyone. I'm mentally. I can't get married to anyone—ever.

## AMERICAN BEAUTY 1999, USA
**Director:** Sam Mendes
**Cast:** Kevin Spacey, Annette Bening, Thora Birch
**Screenplay:** Alan Ball

## EXCALIBUR 1989, USA
**Director:** John Boorman **Cast:** Nicol Williamson, Nigel Terry, Helen Mirren
**Screenplay:** Rospo Pallenberg and John Boorman
*Based on the book by Sir Thomas Malory*

## XANADU 1980, USA
**Director:** Robert Greenwald **Cast:** Olivia Newton-John, Gene Kelly, Michael Beck
**Screenplay:** Richard Christian Danus and Marc Reid Rubel

## DONNIE BRASCO 1997, USA
**Director:** Mike Newell
**Cast:** Al Pacino, Johnny Depp, Michael Madsen
**Screenplay:** Paul Attanasio *Based on the book by Joseph D. Pistone and Richard Woodley*

## PSYCHO 1960, USA
**Director:** Alfred Hitchcook **Cast:** Anthony Perkins, Janet Leigh, Vera Miles
**Screenplay:** Joseph Stefano *Based on the book by Robert Bloch*

## THE THREE FACES OF EVE 1957, USA
**Director:** Nunnally Johnson
**Cast:** Joanne Woodward, David Wayne, Lee J. Cobb
**Screenplay:** Nunnally Johnson
*Based on the book by Corbett Thigpen and Hervey M. Cleckley*

– If I asked you to kill me, would you?
– I don't know. How would I do it? I couldn't live without ya.

– Hold me.
– I can't.

I dunno what the hell's in there, but it's
weird and pissed off, whatever it is.

Dave, this conversation can serve no purpose anymore. Goodbye.

Jane, since I've met you, I've noticed things that I never
knew were there before: birds singing, dew glistening
on a newly formed leaf, stoplights.

There's no reason to become alarmed, and we hope you'll enjoy
the rest of your flight. By the way, is there anyone on board who
knows how to fly a plane?

## SID & NANCY  1986, USA
**Director:** Alex Cox
**Cast:** Gary Oldman, Chloe Webb, Andrew Schofield
**Screenplay:** Alex Cox and Abbe Wool

## EDWARD SCISSORHANDS  1990, USA
**Director:** Tim Burton
**Cast:** Johnny Depp, Winona Ryder, Dianne Wiest
**Screenplay:** Tim Burton and Caroline Thompson

## THE THING  1982, USA
**Director:** John Carpenter
**Cast:** Kurt Russell, Richard Dysart, A. Wilford Brimley
**Screenplay:** John W. Campbell Jr. and Bill Lancaster

## 2001: A SPACE ODYSSEY  1968, United Kingdom
**Director:** Stanley Kubrick
**Cast:** Keir Dullea, William Sylvester, Gary Lockwood
**Screenplay:** Stanley Kubrick and Arthur C. Clarke

## THE NAKED GUN:  FROM THE FILES OF POLICE SQUAD  1988, USA
**Director:** David Zucker
**Cast:** Leslie Nielsen, George Kennedy, Priscilla Presley
**Screenplay:** Jim Abrahams, David Zucker and Pat Proft

## AIRPLANE! / FLYING HIGH  1980, USA
**Director:** Jim Abrahams, David Zucker, Jerry Zucker
**Cast:** Robert Hays, Julie Hagerty, Robert Stack
**Screenplay:** Jim Abrahams, David Zucker and Jerry Zucker

In Sicily, women are more dangerous than shotguns.


Now, ya don't fuck around with the infinite.


Do you think God knew what He was doing when He created woman? Huh? No shit. I really wanna know. Or do you think it was another one of His minor mistakes like tidal waves, earth quakes, FLOODS? You think women are like that? What's the matter? You don't think God makes mistakes? Of course He does. We ALL make mistakes. Of course, when WE make mistakes they call it evil. When GOD makes mistakes, they call it . . . nature. So whaddya think? Women . . . a mistake . . . or DID HE DO IT TO US ON PURPOSE?

Sometimes, you have to lose yourself 'fore you can find anything.


I like big, fat men like you. When they fall they make more noise!


– I hear you have a taste for little boys. Is that not so?
– No, Caesar, big boys.

## THE GODFATHER 1972, USA
**Director:** Francis Ford Coppola
**Cast:** Marlon Brando, Al Pacino, James Caan
**Screenplay:** Mario Puzo and Francis Ford Coppola *Based on the book by Mario Puzo*

## MEAN STREETS 1973, USA
**Director:** Martin Scorsese  **Cast:** Robert De Niro, Harvey Keitel, David Proval
**Screenplay:** Martin Scorsese and Mardik Martin

## THE WITCHES OF EASTWICK 1987, USA
**Director:** George Miller
**Cast:** Jack Nicholson, Cher, Susan Sarandon
**Screenplay:** Michael Cristofe
*Based on the book by John Updike*

## DELIVERANCE 1972, USA
**Director:** John Boorman
**Cast:** Jon Voight, Burt Reynolds, Ned Beatty
**Screenplay:** James Dickey
*Based on the book by James Dickey*

## THE GOOD, THE BAD, AND THE UGLY 1966, Italy
**Director:** Sergio Leone
**Cast:** Clint Eastwood, Lee Van Cleef, Eli Wallach
**Screenplay:** Luciano Vincenzoni, Sergio Leone, Agenore Incrocci and Furio Scarpelli

## CALIGULA 1980, Italy/USA
**Director:** Tinto Brass
**Cast:** Malcolm McDowell, Peter O'Toole, Teresa Ann Savoy
**Screenplay:** Gore Vidal, Bob Guccione, Giancarlo Lui and Franco Rossellini

Don't be alarmed, Ladies and Gentlemen.
Those chains are made of chrome steel.

– And you know what they call a . . . a . . . a Quarter Pounder
with Cheese in Paris?
– They don't call it a Quarter Pounder with cheese?
– No man, they got the metric system. They wouldn't know what the
fuck a Quarter Pounder is.
– Then what do they call it?
– They call it a Royale with cheese.
– A Royale with cheese! What do they call a Big Mac?
– A Big Mac's a Big Mac, but they call it le Big-Mac.
– Le Big-Mac! Ha ha ha ha! What do they call a Whopper?
– I dunno, I didn't go to no Burger King.

I'm afraid. I'm afraid. Dave, Dave, my mind is going. I can feel it.

You have brought music back in to my life. I had forgotten.

I'd like to see you with your pants off, Mr. Reed.

– Hi, man.
– What are you doing?!
– I'm drinking wine and eating cheese,
and catching some rays, you know . . .

## KING KONG 1933, USA
**Directors:** Merian C. Cooper, Ernest B. Schoedsack
**Cast:** Fay Wray, Robert Armstrong, Bruce Cabot
**Screenplay:** James Ashmore Creelman and Ruth Rose

## PULP FICTION 1994, USA
**Director:** Quentin Tarantino
**Cast:** John Travolta, Samuel L. Jackson, Uma Thurman
**Screenplay:** Quentin Tarantino and Roger Avary

## 2001: A SPACE ODYSSEY 1968, United Kingdom
**Director:** Stanley Kubrick **Cast:** Keir Dullea, William Sylvester, Gary Lockwood
**Screenplay:** Stanley Kubrick and Arthur C. Clarke

## THE SOUND OF MUSIC 1965, USA
**Director:** Robert Wise **Cast:** Julie Andrews, Christopher Plummer, Eleanor Parker
**Screenplay:** Ernest Lehman, Richard Rodgers and Oscar Hammerstein II,
     Howard Lindsay and Russel Crouse

## REDS 1981, USA **Director:** Warren Beatty **Cast:** Warren Beatty, Diane
     Keaton, Edward Herrmann **Screenplay:** Warren Beatty, Trevor Griffiths,
     Elaine May, John Reed (II), Jeremy Pikser and Peter S. Feibleman

## KELLY'S HEROES 1970, USA
**Director:** Brian G. Hutton **Cast:** Clint Eastwood, Telly Savalas, Don Rickles
**Screenplay:** Troy Kennedy-Martin

This kind of certainty comes but once in a lifetime.

I only get carsick on boats.

Yes, of course, because all the best people all shave twice a day.

Man, I see in Fight Club the strongest and smartest men who've ever lived. I see all this potential, and I see squandering. God damn it, an entire generation pumping gas, waiting tables; slaves with white collars. Advertising has us chasing cars and clothes, working jobs we hate so we can buy shit we don't need. We're the middle children of history, man. No purpose or place. We have no Great War. No Great Depression. Our Great War's a spiritual war . . . our Great Depression is our lives. We've all been raised on television to believe that one day we'd all be millionaires, and movie gods, and rock stars. But we won't. And we're slowly learning that fact. And we're very, very pissed off.

I pray that I may never see the desert again. Hear me, God.

My idea of Heaven is a solid white nightclub with me as a headliner for all eternity, and they LOVE me.

## THE BRIDGES OF MADISON COUNTY 1995, USA
**Director:** Clint Eastwood  **Cast:** Clint Eastwood, Meryl Streep, Annie Corley
**Screenplay:** Richard LaGravenese  *Based on the book by Robert James Waller*

## MIDNIGHT COWBOY 1969, USA
**Director:** John Schlesinger  **Cast:** Dustin Hoffman, Jon Voight, Sylvia Miles
**Screenplay:** Waldo Salt  *Based on the book by James Leo Herlihy*

## LOLITA 1962, United Kingdom
**Director:** Stanley Kubrick  **Cast:** James Mason, Shelley Winters, Peter Sellers
**Screenplay:** Vladimir Nabokov and Stanley Kubrick
*Based on the book by Vladimir Nabokov*

## FIGHT CLUB 1999, USA
**Director:** David Fincher
**Cast:** Brad Pitt, Edward Norton, Helena Bonham Carter
**Screenplay:** Jim Uhls
*Based on the book by Chuck Palahniuk*

## LAWRENCE OF ARABIA 1962, United Kingdom
**Director:** David Lean
**Cast:** Peter O'Toole, Alec Guinness, Anthony Quinn
**Screenplay:** T.E. Lawrence, Robert Bolt and Michael Wilson

## THE EXORCIST 1973, USA
**Director:** William Friedkin
**Cast:** Ellen Burstyn, Max von Sydow, Linda Blair
**Screenplay:** William Peter Blatty

– I've never seen you take a drink in your life.
– Honey, there are a lot of things you ain't never seen me do.
That's no sign I don't do 'em.


– The wind opens the sea.
– God opens the sea with a blast of his nostrils.


– What would you call that hairstyle you're wearing?
– Arthur.


– At least we've got it stopped.
– Yeah, as long as the Arctic stays cold.


– I don't want to put a wad of white powder in my nose.
There's the nasal membrane . . .
– You never want to try anything new, Alvy.
– How can you say that? Whose idea was it? I said that you, I and
that girl from your acting class should sleep together in a threesome.
– Well, that's sick!
– Yeah, I know it's sick, but it's new. You didn't say it couldn' be sick.

Boys, you got to learn not to talk to nuns that way.

## THE THREE FACES OF EVE 1957, USA
**Director:** Nunnally Johnson
**Cast:** Joanne Woodward, David Wayne, Lee J. Cobb
**Screenplay:** Nunnally Johnson
*Based on the book by Corbett Thigpen and Hervey M. Cleckley*

## THE TEN COMMANDMENTS 1956, USA
**Director:** Cecil B. DeMille
**Cast:** Charlton Heston, Yul Brynner, Anne Baxter
**Screenplay:** J.H. Ingraham, A.E. Southon, Dorothy Clarke Wilson,
    Æneas MacKenzie, Jesse Lasky Jr., Jack Gariss and Fredric M. Frank

## A HARD DAY'S NIGHT 1964, United Kingdom
**Director:** Richard Lester
**Cast:** John Lennon, Paul McCartney, George Harrison
**Screenplay:** Alun Owen

## THE BLOB 1958, USA
**Director:** Irwin S. Yeaworth Jr.
**Cast:** Steve McQueen, Aneta Corsaut, Earl Rowe
**Screenplay:** Kay Linaker, Irvine H. Millgate

## ANNIE HALL 1977, USA
**Director:** Woody Allen
**Cast:** Woody Allen, Diane Keaton, Tony Roberts
**Screenplay:** Woody Allen and Marshall Brickman

## THE BLUES BROTHERS 1980, USA
**Director:** John Landis   **Cast:** John Belushi, Dan Aykroyd, Cab Calloway
**Screenplay:** Dan Aykroyd and John Landis

– Rhett . . . if you go Rhett, where shall I go? What shall I do?
– Frankly, my dear, I don't give a damn.


– This time, John Wayne does not walk off into the sunset
with Grace Kelly.
– That was Gary Cooper, asshole.


– Your tongue is old but sharp, Cicero. Be careful how you wag
it. One day it will cut off your head.


– So, yaw fatha was a Woman? Who was he?
– He was a Centurion, in the Jerusalem Garrisons.
– Weally? What was his name?
– Naughtius Maximus.
– Centuwion, do we have anyone of that name in the gawwison?
– Well, no, sir.
– Well, you sound vewy sure. Have you checked?
– Well, no, sir. Umm, I think it's a joke, sir . . . like, uh,
"Sillius Soddus" or . . . "Biggus Dickus," sir.


The reality is that we do not wash our own laundry.
It just gets dirtier.


The richest man is the one with the most powerful friends.

## GONE WITH THE WIND  1939, USA
**Director:** Victor Fleming  **Cast:** Clark Gable, Vivien Leigh, Leslie Howard
**Screenplay:** Sidney Howard, Ben Hecht, Jo Swerling
*Based on the book by Margaret Mitchell*

## DIE HARD  1988, USA
**Director:** John McTiernan
**Cast:** Bruce Willis, Alan Rickman, Bonnie Bedelia
**Screenplay:** Jeb Stuart and Steven E. de Souza  *Based on the book by Roderick Thorp*

## CLEOPATRA  1963, USA
**Director:** Joseph L. Mankiewicz
**Cast:** Elizabeth Taylor, Richard Burton, Rex Harrison
**Screenplay:** Sidney Buchman, Ben Hecht, Ranald MacDougall and
    Joseph L. Mankiewicz  *Based on the book by Carlo Mario Franzero*

## MONTY PYTHON'S LIFE OF BRIAN  1979, United Kingdom
**Director:** Terry Jones
**Cast:** Graham Chapman, John Cleese, Terry Gilliam
**Screenplay:** Graham Chapman, John Cleese, Terry Gilliam, Eric Idle, Terry Jones
    and Michael Palin

## SERPICO  1973, USA
**Director:** Sidney Lumet  **Cast:** Al Pacino, John Randolph, Jack Kehoe
**Screenplay:** Waldo Salt and Norman Wexler  *Based on the book by Peter Maas*

## THE GODFATHER PART III  1990, USA
**Director:** Francis Ford Coppola  **Cast:** Al Pacino, Diane Keaton, Talia Shire
**Screenplay:** Mario Puzo and Francis Ford Coppola

– I'd like an omelet, plain, and a chicken salad sandwich on wheat toast, no mayonnaise, no butter, no lettuce. And a cup of coffee.
– A #2, chicken salad sand. Hold the butter, the lettuce, the mayonnaise, and a cup of coffee. Anything else?
– Yeah, now all you have to do is hold the chicken, bring me the toast, give me a check for the chicken salad sandwich, and you haven't broken any rules.
– You want me to hold the chicken, huh?
– I want you to hold it between your knees.

I'm gonna make you squeal like a pig. Weeeeeee!

What we do know is that, as the chemical window closed, another awakening took place; that the human spirit is more powerful than any drug—and *that* is what needs to be nourished: with work, play, friendship, family. *These* are the things that matter. This is what we'd forgotten—the simplest things.

– Just how bad is it?
– It's a fire. All fires are bad.

After all . . . tomorrow is another day.

## FIVE EASY PIECES  1970, USA
**Director:** Bob Rafelson
**Cast:** Jack Nicholson, Karen Black, Billy Green Bush
**Screenplay:** Carole Eastman and Bob Rafelson

## DELIVERANCE  1972, USA
**Director:** John Boorman  **Cast:** Jon Voight, Burt Reynolds, Ned Beatty
**Screenplay:** James Dickey  *Based on the book by James Dickey*

## AWAKENINGS  1990, USA
**Director:** Penny Marshall
**Cast:** Robert De Niro, Robin Williams, Julie Kavner
**Screenplay:** Steven Zaillian
*Based on the book by Oliver Sacks*

## THE TOWERING INFERNO  1974, USA
**Director:** John Guillermin, Irwin Allen
**Cast:** Steve McQueen, Paul Newman, William Holden
**Screenplay:** Stirling Silliphant
*Based on the book by Richard Martin Stern, Thomas N. Scortia and Frank M. Robinson*

## GONE WITH THE WIND  1939, USA
**Director:** Victor Fleming  **Cast:** Clark Gable, Vivien Leigh, Leslie Howard
**Screenplay:** Sidney Howard, Ben Hecht, David O. Selznick, Jo
Swerling and John Van Druten  *Based on the book by Margaret Mitchell*

I've been in prison for three years. My dick
gets hard if the wind blows.

I'm tapped out, Marv. American Express's got
a hit man lookin' for me.

– Have you no human consideration?
– Show me a human, and I might have!

– Where am I?
– You're in the records room.
– The records room? Oh, then I'm fine.
– Can I get you something?
– Yeah, do you have the Beatles' *White Album*?
Never mind, just  bring me a cup of hot fat.
And the head of Alfredo Garcia while you're out there.

– You kill anybody?
– A few cops
– No real people?
– Just cops.

## 48 HRS. 1982, USA
**Director:** Walter Hill
**Cast:** Nick Nolte, Eddie Murphy, Annette O'Toole
**Screenplay:** Roger Spottiswoode, Walter Hill, Larry Gross, Steven E. de Souza
  and Jeb Stuart

## WALL STREET 1987, USA
**Director:** Oliver Stone
**Cast:** Michael Douglas, Charlie Sheen, Daryl Hannah
**Screenplay:** Stanley Weiser and Oliver Stone

## ALL ABOUT EVE 1950, USA
**Director:** Joseph L. Mankiewicz
**Cast:** Bette Davis, Anne Baxter, George Sanders
**Screenplay:** Joseph L. Mankiewicz and Mary Orr

## FLETCH 1985, USA
**Director:** Michael Ritchie
**Cast:** Chevy Chase, Dana Wheeler Nicholson, Tim Matheson
**Screenplay:** Andrew Bergman
*Based on the book by Gregory McDonald*

## RESERVOIR DOGS 1992, USA
**Director:** Quentin Tarantino
**Cast:** Harvey Keitel, Tim Roth, Michael Madsen
**Screenplay:** Roger Avary and Quentin Tarantino

. . . and as they both sink beneath the waves, the frog cries out, Why did you sting me, Mr. Scorpion? For now we both will drown! Scorpion replies, I can't help it. It's in my nature!

Winning that ticket, Rose, was the best thing that ever happened to me. It brought me to you. And I'm thankful for that, Rose. I'm thankful. You must do me this honor, Rose. Promise me you'll survive. That you won't give up, no matter what happens, no matter how hopeless. Promise me now, Rose, and never let go of that promise.

– You ever wished you were someone else?
– I'd like to try being Porky Pig.
– I never wanted to be anyone else.

When you're a Jet you're a Jet all the way; from your first cigarette until your last dying day!

– What will we do when we have lost the war?
– Prepare for the next one.

## THE CRYING GAME 1992, United Kingdom
**Director:** Neil Jordan
**Cast:** Stephan Rea, Miranda Richardson, Forest Whitaker
**Screenplay:** Neil Jordan

## TITANIC 1997, USA
**Director:** James Cameron
**Cast:** Leonardo DiCaprio, Kate Winslet, Billy Zane
**Screenplay:** James Cameron

## EASY RIDER 1969, USA
**Director:** Dennis Hopper
**Cast:** Peter Fonda, Dennis Hopper, Jack Nicholson
**Screenplay:** Peter Fonda, Dennis Hopper and Terry Southern

## WEST SIDE STORY 1961, USA
**Director:** Robert Wise, Jerome Robbins
**Cast:** Natalie Wood, Richard Beymer, George Chakiris
**Screenplay:** Jerome Robbins, Arthur Laurents and Ernest Lehman
*Based on the play* Romeo and Juliet *by William Shakespeare*

## CROSS OF IRON 1977, United Kingdom/West Germany
**Director:** Sam Peckinpah
**Cast:** James Coburn, Maximilian Schell, James Mason
**Screenplay:** Julius J. Epstein, James Hamilton and Walter Kelley
*Based on the book by Willi Heinrich*

– Is it safe? Is it safe?

– You're talking to me?

– Is it safe?

– What safe?

– Is it safe?

– I don't know what you mean. I can't tell you something's safe or not, unless I know specifically what you're talking about.

– Is it safe?

– Tell me what it is first.

– Is it safe?

– Yes, it's safe. It's very safe. So safe you wouldn't believe it.

– Is it safe?

– No, it's not safe. It's very dangerous. Be careful.


He won't get far on hot air and fantasy.



Let's have an intelligent conversation here: I'll talk, and you listen.



Stanley, see this? This is this. This ain't something else. This is this. From now on you're on your own.


A prayer's as good as a bayonet on a day like this.

## MARATHON MAN 1976, USA

**Director:** John Schlesinger
**Cast:** Dustin Hoffman, Laurence Olivier, Roy Scheider
**Screenplay:** William Goldman
*Based on the book by William Goldman*

## THE ADVENTURES OF BARON
## MUNCHAUSEN 1989, United Kingdom

**Director:** Terry Gilliam  **Cast:** John Neville, Eric Idle, Sarah Polley
**Screenplay:** Terry Gilliam and Charles McKeown
*Based on the book by Rudolph Erich Raspe*

## WATERWORLD  1995, USA

**Director:** Kevin Reynolds
**Cast:** Kevin Costner, Dennis Hopper, Jeanne Tripplehorn
**Screenplay:** Peter Rader and David Twohy

## THE DEER HUNTER  1978, USA

**Director:** Michael Cimino  **Cast:** Robert De Niro, Christopher Walken, Meryl Streep
**Screenplay:** Michael Cimino, Louis Garfinkle, Quinn K. Redeker and Deric Washburn

## ZULU  1964, United Kingdom

**Director:** Cy Endfield  **Cast:** Stanley Baker, Jack Hawkins, Ulla Jacobsson
**Screenplay:** John Prebble and Cy Endfield

You can't fight in here. This is the War Room!

– Play it once, Sam. For old time's sake.
– I don't know what you mean, Miss Ilsa.
– Play it, Sam. Play "As Time Goes By."

– You said bullshit and experience is all it takes, right?
– Right.
– Come on in and experience some of my bullshit.

A guy told me one time, "Don't let youself get attached to anything you are not willing to walk out on in thirty seconds flat if you feel the heat around the corner."

– Henry, I have some reports here from your Major O'Houlihan that I, frankly, find hard to believe.
– Well, don't believe them then, General. Good-bye.

## DR. STRANGELOVE OR: HOW I LEARNED TO STOP WORRYING AND LOVE THE BOMB 1964, USA

**Director:** Stanley Kubrick
**Cast:** Peter Sellers, George C. Scott, Sterling Hayden
**Screenplay:** Stanley Kubrick, Terry Southern and Peter George III
*Based on the book by Peter George*

## CASABLANCA 1942, USA

**Director:** Michael Curtiz
**Cast:** Humphrey Bogart, Ingrid Bergman, Paul Henreid
**Screenplay:** Murray Burnett, Joan Alison, Julius J. Epstein, Philip G. Epstein,
    Howard Koch and Casey Robinson

## 48 HRS. 1982, USA

**Director:** Walter Hill
**Cast:** Nick Nolte, Eddie Murphy, Annette O'Toole
**Screenplay:** Roger Spottiswoode, Walter Hill, Larry Gross, Steven E. de Souza
    and Jeb Stuart

## HEAT 1995, USA

**Director:** Michael Mann
**Cast:** Al Pacino, Robert De Niro, Val Kilmer
**Screenplay:** Michael Mann

## MASH 1970, USA

**Director:** Robert Altman
**Cast:** Donald Sutherland, Elliott Gould, Tom Skerritt
**Screenplay:** Ring Lardner Jr.
*Based on the book by Richard Hooker*

– Why am I Mr. Pink?
– Because you're a faggot, alright?

I don't feel I have to wipe everybody out,
Tom. Just my enemies.

We can't bury Cheryl. She's our friend.

E.T. phone home.

– What kind of childhood did you have?
– Short.

## RESERVOIR DOGS 1992, USA
**Director:** Quentin Tarantino
**Cast:** Harvey Keitel, Tim Roth, Michael Madsen
**Screenplay:** Roger Avary and Quentin Tarantino

## THE GODFATHER PART II 1974, USA
**Director:** Francis Ford Coppola
**Cast:** Al Pacino, Robert De Niro, Robert Duvall
**Screenplay:** Mario Puzo and Francis Ford Coppola

## THE EVIL DEAD 1983, USA
**Director:** Sam Raimi
**Cast:** Bruce Campbell, Ellen Sandweiss, Hal Delrich
**Screenplay:** Sam Raimi

## E.T. THE EXTRATERRESTRIAL 1982, USA
**Director:** Steven Spielberg
**Cast:** Dee Wallace, Henry Thomas, Peter Coyote
**Screenplay:** Melissa Mathison

## ESCAPE FROM ALCATRAZ 1979, USA
**Director:** Donald Siegel
**Cast:** Clint Eastwood, Patrick McGoohan, Roberts Blossom
**Screenplay:** Richard Tuggle
*Based on the book by J. Campbell Bruce*

Where the Lord closes a door,
somewhere He opens a window.

Well, we went skinny dipping, and we
did things that frightened the fish.

You're like the thief who isn't the least bit sorry he stole,
but is terribly, terribly sorry he's going to jail.

Disturbing the peace? I got thrown out of a window!
What's the fucking charge for getting pushed
out of a moving car, huh? Jaywalking?!

Martha, in my mind, you're buried in cement right up
to the neck. No, up to the nose, it's much quieter.

## THE SOUND OF MUSIC 1965, USA
**Director:** Robert Wise
**Cast:** Julie Andrews, Christopher Plummer, Eleanor Parker
**Screenplay:** Ernest Lehman, Richard Rodgers and Oscar Hammerstein II, Howard Lindsay and Russel Crouse

## STEEL MAGNOLIAS 1989, USA
**Director:** Herbert Ross
**Cast:** Sally Field, Dolly Parton, Julia Roberts
**Screenplay:** Robert Harling

## GONE WITH THE WIND 1939, USA
**Director:** Victor Fleming
**Cast:** Clark Gable, Vivien Leigh, Leslie Howard
**Screenplay:** Sidney Howard, Ben Hecht, David O. Selznick, Jo Swerling and John Van Druten
*Based on the book by Margaret Mitchell*

## BEVERLY HILLS COP 1984, USA
**Director:** Martin Brest
**Cast:** Eddie Murphy, Judge Reinhold, John Ashton
**Screenplay:** Danilo Bach and Daniel Petrie Jr.

## WHO'S AFRAID OF VIRGINIA WOOLF? 1966, USA
**Director:** Mike Nichols
**Cast:** Elizabeth Taylor, Richard Burton, George Segal
**Screenplay:** Edward Albee and Ernest Lehman

– You don't know how hard it is being a woman looking the way I do.
– You don't know how hard it is being a man looking at the woman looking the way you do.

There are never enough hours in the days of a queen, and her nights have too many.

Generally, you don't see that kind of behavior in a major appliance.

If he'd just pay me what he's spending to make me stop robbing him, I'd stop robbing him.

A repo man spends his life getting into tense situations.

## WHO FRAMED ROGER RABBIT 1988, USA
**Director:** Robert Zemeckis
**Cast:** Bob Hoskins, Christopher Lloyd, Joanna Cassidy
**Screenplay:** Jeffrey Price and Peter S. Seaman
*Based on the book by Gary K. Wolf*

## CLEOPATRA 1963, USA
**Director:** Joseph L. Mankiewicz
**Cast:** Elizabeth Taylor, Richard Burton, Rex Harrison
**Screenplay:** Sidney Buchman, Ben Hecht, Ranald MacDougall and
Joseph L. Mankiewicz
*Based on the book by Carlo Mario Franzero*

## GHOSTBUSTERS 1984, USA
**Director:** Ivan Reitman
**Cast:** Bill Murray, Dan Aykroyd, Harold Ramis
**Screenplay:** Dan Aykroyd, Harold Ramis and Rick Moranis

## BUTCH CASSIDY AND THE SUNDANCE KID 1969, USA
**Director:** George Roy Hill
**Cast:** Paul Newman, Robert Redford, Katharine Ross
**Screenplay:** William Goldman

## REPO MAN 1984, USA
**Director:** Alex Cox
**Cast:** Emilio Estevez, Harry Dean Stanton, Vonetta McGee
**Screenplay:** Alex Cox

Sorry boys, all the stitches in the world can't sew me together again.

– What have you been doing all these years?
– I've been going to bed early.

It's Halloween! Everyone's entitled to one good scare.

Meyer, we have known each other since we were too young to fuck.

Just because some kid smacks into your wife on the turnpike
doesn't make it a crime to be seventeen years old.

## CARLITO'S WAY 1993, USA
**Director:** Brian De Palma
**Cast:** Al Pacino, Sean Penn, Penelope Ann Miller
**Screenplay:** David Koepp
*Based on the book by Edwin Torres*

## ONCE UPON A TIME IN AMERICA 1984, USA
**Director:** Sergio Leone
**Cast:** Robert De Niro, James Woods, Elizabeth McGovern
**Screenplay:** Leonardo Benvenuti, Piero De Bernardi, Enrico Medioli, Franco Arcalli, Franco Ferrini, Sergio Leone, Stuart Kaminsky and Ernesto Gastaldi
*Based on the book by Harry Grey (II)*

## HALLOWEEN 1978, USA
**Director:** John Carpenter
**Cast:** Donald Pleasence, Jamie Lee Curtis
**Screenplay:** John Carpenter and Debra Hill

## BUGSY 1991, USA
**Director:** Barry Levinson
**Cast:** Warren Beatty, Annette Bening, Harvey Keitel
**Screenplay:** James Toback *Based on the book by Dean Jennings*

## THE BLOB 1958, USA
**Director:** Irwin S. Yeaworth Jr.
**Cast:** Steve McQueen, Aneta Corsaut, Earl Rowe
**Screenplay:** Kay Linaker, Irvine H. Millgate

Boards don't hit back.

– Hippy, you think everything is a conspiracy.
– Everything is.

Frankly, you're beginning to smell, and for
a stud in New York, that's a handicap.

– Do you believe in God?
– The question is: does God believe in me?

I know, I know. We are your chosen people. But,
once in a while, can't you choose someone else?

Well, I don't like to see things goin' good or bad.
I like 'em in between.

## ENTER THE DRAGON 1973, USA
**Director:** Robert Clouse
**Cast:** Bruce Lee, John Saxon, Jim Kelly
**Screenplay:** Michael Allin

## THE ABYSS 1989, USA
**Director:** James Cameron
**Cast:** Ed Harris, Mary Elizabeth Mastrantonio, Michael Biehn
**Screenplay:** James Cameron

## MIDNIGHT COWBOY 1969, USA
**Director:** John Schlesinger
**Cast:** Dustin Hoffman, Jon Voight, Sylvia Miles
**Screenplay:** Waldo Salt
*Based on the book by James Leo Herlihy*

## LOLITA 1962, United Kingdom
**Director:** Stanley Kubrick
**Cast:** James Mason, Shelley Winters, Peter Sellers
**Screenplay:** Vladimir Nabokov and Stanley Kubrick
*Based on the book by Vladimir Nabokov*

## FIDDLER ON THE ROOF 1971, USA
**Director:** Norman Jewison
**Cast:** (Chaim) Topol, Norma Crane, Leonard Frey
**Screenplay:** Joseph Stein
*Based on the book by Sholom Aleichem*

## RED RIVER 1948, USA
**Director:** Howard Hawks
**Cast:** John Wayne, Montgomery Clift, Walter Brennan
**Screenplay:** Borden Chase and Charles Schnee

I do wish we could chat longer,
but I'm having an old friend for dinner. Bye.

– Is this where you live?
– Who lives?

I'm the best you ever seen, Fats. I'm the best there is.
Even if you beat me, I'm still the best.

That's too bad. I was going to marry her. I already
put a deposit on twin cemetery plots.

It only took me one night to realize if brains
were dynamite, you couldn't blow your nose.

Never! I'll never turn to the Dark Side! You've failed,
your highness. I am a Jedi, like my father before me.

## THE SILENCE OF THE LAMBS 1991, USA
**Director:** Jonathan Demme
**Cast:** Jodie Foster, Anthony Hopkins, Scott Glenn
**Screenplay:** Ted Tally
*Based on the book by Thomas Harris*

## REBEL WITHOUT A CAUSE 1955, USA
**Director:** Nicholas Ray
**Cast:** James Dean, Natalie Wood, Sal Mineo
**Screenplay:** Nicholas Ray, Irving Shulman and Stewart Stern

## THE HUSTLER 1961, USA
**Director:** Robert Rossen
**Cast:** Paul Newman, Jackie Gleason, Piper Laurie
**Screenplay:** Sidney Carroll and Robert Rossen
*Based on the book by Walter Tevis*

## WHAT'S UP, TIGER LILY? 1966, Japan
**Director:** Senkichi Taniguchi
**Cast:** Tatsuya Mihashi, Mie Hama, Akiko Wakabayashi
**Screenplay:** Woody Allen, Julie Bennett, Frank Buxton, Louise Lasser,
    Len Maxwell, Mickey Rose and Bryan Wilson

## AMERICAN GRAFFITI 1973, USA
**Director:** George Lucas
**Cast:** Richard Dreyfuss, Ron Howard, Paul Le Mat
**Screenplay:** George Lucas, Gloria Katz and Willard Huyck

## RETURN OF THE JEDI 1983, USA
**Director:** Richard Marquand
**Cast:** Mark Hamill, Harrison Ford, Carrie Fisher
**Screenplay:** George Lucas and Lawrence Kasdan

– How do you feel?
– Like the kling klang king of the rim ram room.

The only arithmetic he ever got was hearing
the referee count up to ten.

He's more machine now than man; twisted and evil.

Does the noise in my head bother you?

Seven schools in seven states and the only
thing different is my locker combination.

You give me powders, pills, baths, injections,
enemas—when all I need is love.

## LEAVING LAS VEGAS   1995, USA
**Director:** Mike Figgis
**Cast:** Nicolas Cage, Elisabeth Shue, Julian Sands
**Screenplay:** Mike Figgis
*Based on the book by John O'Brien*


## ON THE WATERFRONT   1954, USA
**Director:** Elia Kazan
**Cast:** Marlon Brando, Karl Malden, Rod Steiger
**Screenplay:** Bud Schulberg


## RETURN OF THE JEDI   1983, USA
**Director:** Richard Marquand
**Cast:** Mark Hamill, Harrison Ford, Carrie Fisher
**Screenplay:** George Lucas and Lawrence Kasdan


## THE GODS MUST BE CRAZY   1981, Norway
**Director:** Jamie Uys
**Cast:** Marius Weyers, Sandra Prinsloo, N!xau
**Screenplay:** Jamie Uys


## HEATHERS   1989, USA
**Director:** Michael Lehmann
**Cast:** Winona Ryder, Christian Slater, Shannen Doherty
**Screenplay:** Daniel Waters


## THE BRIDGE ON THE RIVER KWAI   1957, United Kingdom
**Director:** David Lean
**Cast:** William Holden, Alec Guinness, Jack Hawkins
**Screenplay:** Michael Wilson, Carl Foreman
*Based on the book by Pierre Boulle*

I'm just a sweet transvestite from Transsexual Transylvania.

Sometimes I don't know where the bullshit ends
and the truth begins.

First learn stand, then learn fly.
Nature's rule, Daniel-san, not mine.

Now listen to me, all of you. You are all condemned men.
We keep you alive to serve this ship. So row well, and live.

– There's been a lamp burning in the window for ya, honey . . . here.
– Oh, I jumped out that window a long time ago.

I'm going next. So if ole' fat ass gets stuck,
I won't get stuck behind her!

## THE ROCKY HORROR PICTURE SHOW 1975, USA
**Director:** Jim Sharman
**Cast:** Tim Curry, Susan Sarandon, Barry Bostwick
**Screenplay:** Richard O'Brien, Jim Sharman

## ALL THAT JAZZ 1979, USA
**Director:** Bob Fosse
**Cast:** Roy Scheider, Jessica Lange, Ann Reinking
**Screenplay:** Robert Alan Aurthur and Bob Fosse

## THE KARATE KID 1984, USA
**Director:** John G. Avildsen
**Cast:** Ralph Macchio, Noriyuki Morita, Elisabeth Shue
**Screenplay:** Robert Mark Kamen

## BEN-HUR 1959, USA
**Director:** William Wyler
**Cast:** Charlton Heston, Jack Hawkins, Stephen Boyd
**Screenplay:** Karl Tunberg, Maxwell Anderson, Christopher Fry and Gore Vidal
*Based on the book by Lew Wallace*

## HIS GIRL FRIDAY 1940, USA
**Director:** Howard Hawks
**Cast:** Cary Grant, Rosalind Russell, Ralph Bellamy
**Screenplay:** Ben Hecht, Charles MacArthur and Charles Lederer

## THE POSEIDON ADVENTURE 1972, USA
**Director:** Ronald Neame
**Cast:** Gene Hackman, Ernest Borgnine, Red Buttons
**Screenplay:** Wendell Mayes and Stirling Silliphant
*Based on the book by Paul Gallico*

Just when I thought that I was out they pull me back in.


Which one of you nuts has got any guts?


No matter what anybody tells you,
words and ideas can change the world.


All those moments will be lost in time, like tears in rain.


Don't kid yourself, Francesca.
You are anything but a simple woman.


I'm young, I'm handsome, I'm fast,
I'm pretty and can't possibly be beat.

## THE GODFATHER PART III 1990, USA
**Director:** Francis Ford Coppola
**Cast:** Al Pacino, Diane Keaton, Talia Shire
**Screenplay:** Mario Puzo and Francis Ford Coppola

## ONE FLEW OVER THE CUCKOO'S NEST 1975, USA
**Director:** Milos Forman
**Cast:** Jack Nicholson, Louise Fletcher, Brad Dourif
**Screenplay:** Bo Goldman and Lawrence Hauben
*Based on the book by Ken Kesey*

## DEAD POETS SOCIETY 1989, USA
**Director:** Peter Weir
**Cast:** Robin Williams, Robert Sean Leonard, Ethan Hawke
**Screenplay:** Tom Schulman

## BLADE RUNNER 1982, USA
**Director:** Ridley Scott
**Cast:** Harrison Ford, Rutger Hauer, Sean Young
**Screenplay:** Hampton Fancher, David Webb Peoples, Roland Kibbee
*Based on the book by Philip K. Dick*

## THE BRIDGES OF MADISON COUNTY 1995, USA
**Director:** Clint Eastwood
**Cast:** Clint Eastwood, Meryl Streep, Annie Corley
**Screenplay:** Richard LaGravenese
*Based on the book by Robert James Waller*

## WHEN WE WERE KINGS 1996, USA
**Director:** Leon Gast
**Cast:** Muhammad Ali, George Foreman, Don King

Might as well call it white jack!

That's funny. That plane's dustin' crops where there ain't no crops.

Made it, Ma! Top of the world!

When a man says "no" to Champagne, he says "no" to life.

Well, I'm sure I'd feel much worse if I weren't
under such heavy sedation.

Toto, I've got a feeling we're not in Kansas anymore.

## OCEAN'S ELEVEN 1960, USA
**Director:** Lewis Milestone
**Cast:** Frank Sinatra, Dean Martin, Sammy Davis Jr.
**Screenplay:** George Clayton Johnson, Jack Golden Russell, Harry Brown,
    Charles Lederer and Billy Wilder

## NORTH BY NORTHWEST 1959, USA
**Director:** Alfred Hitchcock
**Cast:** Cary Grant, Eva Marie Saint, James Mason
**Screenplay:** Ernest Lehman

## WHITE HEAT 1949, USA
**Director:** Raoul Walsh
**Cast:** James Cagney, Virginia Mayo, Edmond O'Brien
**Screenplay:** Virginia Kellogg, Ivan Goff and Ben Roberts

## THE DEER HUNTER 1978, USA
**Director:** Michael Cimino
**Cast:** Robert De Niro, Christopher Walken, Meryl Streep
**Screenplay:** Michael Cimino, Louis Garfinkle, Quinn K. Redeker
    and Deric Washburn

## THIS IS SPINAL TAP 1984, USA
**Director:** Rob Reiner
**Cast:** Michael McKean, Christopher Guest, Harry Shearer
**Screenplay:** Christopher Guest, Michael McKean, Rob Reiner and Harry Shearer

## THE WIZARD OF OZ 1939, USA
**Director:** Victor Fleming
**Cast:** Judy Garland, Ray Bolger, Bert Lahr
**Screenplay:** Noel Langley, Florence Ryerson and Edgar Allan Woolf
*Based on the book by L. Frank Baum*

There's nothing more life-affirming than
getting the shit kicked outta ya.

Who the fuck am I? I'm a, a spoke on a wheel.
And so was he, and so are you.

Twenty dwarves took turns doing handstands on the carpet.

Sweetheart, you can't buy the necessities of life with cookies.

They asked me if I'd seen any strangers in the neighborhood.

You get what you settle for.

## DRUGSTORE COWBOY  1989, USA
**Director:** Gus Van Sant
**Cast:** Matt Dillon, Kelly Lynch, James Remar
**Screenplay:** Gus Van Sant, Daniel Yost and William S. Burroughs
*Based on the book by James Fogle*

## DONNIE BRASCO  1997, USA
**Director:** Mike Newell
**Cast:** Al Pacino, Johnny Depp, Michael Madsen
**Screenplay:** Paul Attanasio
*Based on the book by Joseph D. Pistone and Richard Woodley*

## BUGSY  1991, USA
**Director:** Barry Levinson
**Cast:** Warren Beatty, Annette Bening, Harvey Keitel
**Screenplay:** James Toback.
*Based on the book by Dean Jennings*

## EDWARD SCISSORHANDS  1990, USA
**Director:** Tim Burton
**Cast:** Johnny Depp, Winona Ryder, Dianne Wiest
**Screenplay:** Tim Burton and Caroline Thompson

## CLOSE ENCOUNTERS OF THE THIRD KIND  1977, USA
**Director:** Steven Spielberg
**Cast:** Richard Dreyfuss, François Truffaut, Teri Garr
**Screenplay:** Steven Spielberg, Hal Barwood, Jerry Belson, John Hill
    and Matthew Robbins

## THELMA & LOUISE  1991, USA
**Director:** Ridley Scott
**Cast:** Susan Sarandon, Geena Davis, Harvey Keitel
**Screenplay:** Callie Khouri

. . . Nothing more foolish than a man chasin' his hat.

God made men. Men made slaves.

This whole world's wild at heart and weird on top.

I'll never look like Barbie. Barbie doesn't have bruises.

The only thing I'll ever lay is a rug!

The Force can have a strong influence on the weak-minded.

## MILLER'S CROSSING 1990, USA
**Director:** Joel Coen
**Cast:** Gabriel Byrne, Albert Finney, Marcia Gay Harden
**Screenplay:** Joel Coen and Ethan Coen
*Based on the book by Dashiell Hammett*

## THE TEN COMMANDMENTS 1956, USA
**Director:** Cecil B. DeMille
**Cast:** Charlton Heston, Yul Brynner, Anne Baxter
**Screenplay:** J.H. Ingraham, A.E. Southon, Dorothy Clarke Wilson,
Æneas MacKenzie, Jesse Lasky Jr., Jack Gariss and Fredric M. Frank

## WILD AT HEART 1990, USA
**Director:** David Lynch
**Cast:** Nicolas Cage, Laura Dern, Diane Ladd
**Screenplay:** David Lynch
*Based on the book by Barry Gifford*

## SID & NANCY 1986, USA
**Director:** Alex Cox
**Cast:** Gary Oldman, Chloe Webb, Andrew Schofield
**Screenplay:** Alex Cox and Abbe Wool

## ROCK 'N' ROLL HIGH SCHOOL 1979, USA
**Director:** Allan Arkush, Joe Dante
**Cast:** P.J. Soles, Vincent Van Patten, Clint Howard
**Screenplay:** Richard Whitley, Russ Dvonch

## STAR WARS 1977, USA
**Director:** George Lucas
**Cast:** Mark Hamill, Harrison Ford, Carrie Fisher
**Screenplay:** George Lucas

The best goodbyes are short. Adieu.

I'm too old for this shit!

In case I forget to tell you later—I had a really good time tonight.

I swear to GOD, George, if you ever EXISTED I'd divorce you.

Just like a Wop to bring a knife to a gunfight.

Cyborgs don't feel pain. I do. Don't do that again.

## THE MALTESE FALCON 1941, USA
**Director:** John Huston
**Cast:** Humphrey Bogart, Mary Astor, Peter Lorre
**Screenplay:** John Huston
*Based on the book by Dashiell Hammett*

## LETHAL WEAPON 1987, USA
**Director:** Richard Donner
**Cast:** Mel Gibson, Danny Glover, Gary Busey
**Screenplay:** Shane Black

## PRETTY WOMAN 1990, USA
**Director:** Garry Marshall
**Cast:** Richard Gere, Julia Roberts, Ralph Bellamy
**Screenplay:** J.F. Lawton

## WHO'S AFRAID OF VIRGINIA WOOLF? 1966, USA
**Director:** Mike Nichols
**Cast:** Elizabeth Taylor, Richard Burton, George Segal
**Screenplay:** Edward Albee and Ernest Lehman

## THE UNTOUCHABLES 1987, USA
**Director:** Brian De Palma
**Cast:** Kevin Costner, Sean Connery, Charles Martin Smith
**Screenplay:** David Mamet
*Based on the book by Oscar Fraley and Eliot Ness and Paul Robsky*

## THE TERMINATOR 1984, USA
**Director:** James Cameron
**Cast:** Arnold Schwartzenegger, Michael Biehn, Linda Hamilton
**Screenplay:** James Cameron, Gale Anne Hurd, William Wisher Jr.
and Harlan Ellison

We seem to be made to suffer. It's our lot in life.


Pain can be controlled; you just disconnect it.


I'm just a mean green mother from outer space and I'm bad!


Uh, well, sir, I ain't a f'real cowboy. But I am one helluva stud!


The Duke? The Duke of New York,
A-Number-1, the Big Man, that's who!


To be on the wire is life. The rest is waiting.

## STAR WARS 1977, USA
**Director:** George Lucas
**Cast:** Mark Hamill, Harrison Ford, Carrie Fisher
**Screenplay:** George Lucas

## THE TERMINATOR 1984, USA
**Director:** James Cameron
**Cast:** Arnold Schwartzenegger, Michael Biehn, Linda Hamilton
**Screenplay:** James Cameron, Gale Anne Hurd, William Wisher Jr. and Harlan Ellison

## LITTLE SHOP OF HORRORS 1986, USA
**Director:** Frank Oz
**Cast:** Rick Moranis, Ellen Greene, Vincent Gardenia
**Screenplay:** Charles B. Griffith and Howard Ashman

## MIDNIGHT COWBOY 1969, USA
**Director:** John Schlesinger
**Cast:** Dustin Hoffman, Jon Voight, Sylvia Miles
**Screenplay:** Waldo Salt
*Based on the book by James Leo Herlihy*

## ESCAPE FROM NEW YORK 1981, USA
**Director:** John Carpenter
**Cast:** Kurt Russell, Lee Van Cleef, Ernest Borgnine
**Screenplay:** John Carpenter and Nick Castle

## ALL THAT JAZZ 1979, USA
**Director:** Bob Fosse
**Cast:** Roy Scheider, Jessica Lange, Ann Reinking
**Screenplay:** Robert Alan Aurthur and Bob Fosse

He knew the risks. He didn't have to be there.
It rains, you get wet.

You know what the Queen said? "If I had balls, I'd be King."

Some places are like people: some shine and some don't.

When they come . . . they come at what you love.

Wax on, wax off . . .

Divine decadence darling!

## HEAT  1995, USA
**Director:** Michael Mann
**Cast:** Al Pacino, Robert De Niro, Val Kilmer
**Screenplay:** Michael Mann

## MEAN STREETS  1973, USA
**Director:** Martin Scorsese
**Cast:** Robert De Niro, Harvey Keitel, David Proval
**Screenplay:** Martin Scorsese and Mardik Martin

## THE SHINING  1980, USA
**Director:** Stanley Kubrick
**Cast:** Jack Nicholson, Shelley Duvall, Danny Lloyd
**Screenplay:** Stanley Kubrick and Diane Johnson
*Based on the book by Stephen King*

## THE GODFATHER PART III  1990, USA
**Director:** Francis Ford Coppola
**Cast:** Al Pacino, Diane Keaton, Talia Shire
**Screenplay:** Mario Puzo and Francis Ford Coppola

## THE KARATE KID  1984, USA
**Director:** John G. Avildsen
**Cast:** Ralph Macchio, Noriyuki Morita, Elisabeth Shue
**Screenplay:** Robert Mark Kamen

## CABARET  1972, USA
**Director:** Bob Fosse
**Cast:** Liza Minnelli, Michael York, Helmut Griem
**Screenplay:** John Van Druten, Joe Masteroff and Jay Presson Allen
*Based on the book by Christopher Isherwood*

Play it cool, boy. Real cool.

Get busy living, or get busy dying.

Jesus, what did the old man trade for
these assholes, a used puck bag?

You're tearing me apart!

. . . It ain't like it used to be, but it'll do.

They laughed at me, Mama.

## WEST SIDE STORY 1961, USA
**Director:** Robert Wise, Jerome Robbins
**Cast:** Natalie Wood, Richard Beymer, George Chakiris
**Screenplay:** Jerome Robbins, Arthur Laurents and Ernest Lehman
*Based on* Romeo and Juliet *by William Shakespeare*

## THE SHAWSHANK REDEMPTION 1994, USA
**Director:** Frank Darabont
**Cast:** Tim Robbins, Morgan Freeman, Bob Gunton
**Screenplay:** Frank Darabont
*Based on the book by Stephen King*

## SLAP SHOT 1977, USA
**Director:** George Roy Hill
**Cast:** Paul Newman, Michael Ontkean, Lindsay Crouse
**Screenplay:** Nancy Dowd

## REBEL WITHOUT A CAUSE 1955, USA
**Director:** Nicholas Ray
**Cast:** James Dean, Natalie Wood, Sal Mineo
**Screenplay:** Nicholas Ray, Irving Shulman and Stewart Stern

## THE WILD BUNCH 1969, USA
**Director:** Sam Peckinpah
**Cast:** William Holden, Ernest Borgnine, Robert Ryan
**Screenplay:** Walon Green and Sam Peckinpah

## CARRIE 1976, USA
**Director:** Brian De Palma
**Cast:** Sissy Spacek, Piper Laurie, William Katt
**Screenplay:** Lawrence D. Cohen
*Based on the book by Stephen King*

# INDEX